LET J. PAUL GETTY
TELL YOU...

- How to revolutionize your entire life through satisfying social relationships, engrossing work, stimulating hobbies

- How to prepare yourself *psychologically* for your later years

- What being in good physical condition can do for you

- How to avoid the pitfalls of insufficient economic planning

- What to do about savings accounts, real estate investments, insurance, stocks and bonds

> *"The Golden Age*
> is full of good counsel
> and encouraging ideas."
> —Irving Peck,
> *United Press International*

> "A remarkably practical and
> workable blueprint for a better,
> more secure and more meaningful life."
> —*The State*, Columbia, S.C.

THE GOLDEN AGE
was originally published by Trident Press.

Also by J. Paul Getty

How To Be Rich

Published by Pocket Books

J. PAUL GETTY

THE GOLDEN AGE

PUBLISHED BY POCKET BOOKS NEW YORK

THE GOLDEN AGE

Trident Press edition published April, 1968

A *Pocket Book* edition
1st printing .... June, 1969

This *Pocket Book* edition includes every word
contained in the original, higher-priced edition. It is printed
from brand-new plates made from completely reset, clear, easy-to-read
type. *Pocket Book* editions are published by Pocket Books, a division
of Simon & Schuster, Inc., 630 Fifth Avenue, New York, N.Y. 10020.
Trademarks registered in the United States and other countries.

To the memory of my beloved mother and father,
Sarah C. and George F. Getty

TABLE OF CONTENTS

THE
GOLDEN
AGE

1 A TALE OF TWO CENTURIES

On defining the meaning of the verb "to live." To many of our eighteenth-century forebears, living was a fine art, and they were connoisseurs, savoring life to the full. Our present era offers vast numbers of men and women the opportunity to be "connoisseurs of the art of living" yet, without valid reason, many fail to recognize the possibilities or realize the potentials. But, for tens of millions, our Affluent Age could be—and should be—a truly Golden Age.

Ask yourself, or any number of people chosen at random, to define the verb "to live."

But you had better be warned beforehand: the question is not nearly as simple as it sounds.

"To live" has many, widely disparate shades of meaning. Even the greatly abridged "Concise Edition" of *Webster's New World Dictionary* lists nine primary and two secondary senses in which the verb may be used. Among the primary definitions are these three:

> *To be alive; have life . . .*
> *To remain alive . . .*
> *To enjoy a full and varied life . . .*

11

I'll hazard an educated guess that most replies would hew close to either or both of the first two definitions cited above and that answers even remotely approaching the third would be rare exceptions.

On its face, all this might well appear to be nothing more than a grade-school-level exercise in semantics. But "to enjoy a full and varied life" is not merely a dictionary definition. It is—or most certainly should be—the primary aim and purpose of human existence.

While acknowledging—and wholeheartedly condemning—the ugly imperfections and inequities that continue to mar and scar the American scene, I nonetheless think it valid to generalize that our present era and society offer the average individual unprecedented opportunities for living life to the utmost. Despite any and all shortcomings, *most* of our citizens are better off today than ever before. They are healthier, live longer, enjoy more social justice and equality, are better educated, have more leisure time and are more prosperous than any previous generations of Americans. Within their reach are myriads of conveniences and luxuries that ease the burden of their labors, increase their comfort or simply add more gloss to a society already glittering with unparalleled affluence.

By all logical rules and standards, it should follow that our exceptionally fortunate tens of millions are deriving commensurately greater gratification, fulfillment and serenity from life, but the rules seem to have been annulled and the standards discarded. We are daily told—and presented with much supporting evidence—that our young are disenchanted and disgruntled, our old feel rootless and rejected, and those of our fellows in intermediate age groups are bored and bewildered, unsatisfied and unhappy. The impartial observer is left to ponder the irony that large segments of a society that handily masters the most complex secrets of science and technology are incapable of mastering the techniques of the art of living.

Paradoxically, these techniques were readily grasped and utilized by past, considerably less lavishly endowed generations.

For example, compared to us, our ancestors who lived in eighteenth-century Europe—during the "Age of Enlightenment"—were connoisseurs in the art of living. They understood that their existence had to have depth and dimension and be multifaceted in order to provide them with a sense of gratification, of having fulfilled their human roles.

If they were of the middle or upper classes, our eighteenth-century forebears read good books, listened to good music, admired—and, when they could, collected—good paintings, furniture and objets d'art. They wrote long, interesting letters and, in many instances, fascinating memoirs. They savored a wide range of interests and pursuits—practical, intellectual, cultural and recreational. Somehow, they even managed to find time to linger long hours over good meals spiced with witty conversation.

Of course, when referring to that era, the phrase "if they were of the middle or upper classes" is significant, delineating the prerequisites for entry into a select circle that formed an extremely thin crust atop the eighteenth-century population pie.

But there is no such rigid social stratification in our day. Furthermore, a large—even major—segment of our populace possesses not only the potentials and qualifications but also numberless additional advantages and facilities for becoming "connoisseurs in the art of living."

In the 1960s, skilled laborers, salesmen, bottom-rung executives—people in countless "ordinary" occupations and positions—have as much basic education, leisure time and actual buying power as most members of the eighteenth-century middle classes.

When it comes to intelligence, attractiveness and affluence, a modern-day secretary, nurse or housewife is quite likely to be the equal—or better—of the run-of-the-*salon* middle-class ladies of the 1700s.

As for successful business or professional men and women or upper-bracket executives, it is no exaggeration to suggest that they stand on a starting line par with a fair portion of the eighteenth century's "upper classes"—landowners, important merchants, lesser nobility and the like.

In the Age of Enlightenment, a privileged minority understood that "to live" was to "enjoy a full and varied life"—and did precisely that.

In the Age of Affluence, instead of an elite handful, there

are tens of millions of men and women who could do the same—and even more and better.

Our contemporary society's crying need is to master the art of living—not, of course, in ways and fashions identical to those characteristic of the 1700s, but surely on no lesser scales and to no lesser degrees.

Naturally, tastes and preferences vary. What specific "mix" of interests and activities will provide a life sufficiently full and varied to satisfy you or the next person is entirely a matter of personal choice and inclination. One person may abhor Boucher and Browning and dote on tennis and the theater. Another may prefer outdoor sports to observing the stars even while he would rather play pool than read poetry.

I myself have been an active, successful businessman for well over fifty years. During that period, my holdings and enterprises have grown in size and multiplied in number, and the attendant problems and responsibilities increased by logarithmic proportions.

Nonetheless, and notwithstanding all the demands made on my time and energies, I have consistently striven to live a rounded existence, to avoid becoming bogged down in a narrow groove and acquiring what I have heard aptly called "tunnel vision." Any such one-dimensional course would, I am sure, have proved fatal to my career—to say nothing of my individuality.

I began developing other, nonbusiness interests and engaging in a reasonably broad range of "extracurricular" activities early in my career. These have all had a profoundly salutary effect, for each helped generate enthusiasm for the next, and all added zest to life and, what is more, helped me to be a better, more energetic and efficient businessman and a much more content and happy person.

I am hardly an exception or exceptional. I know many individuals in many different fields and occupations who hold similar views and have formed similar patterns. All say and show that they have benefited greatly, gaining broader perspectives, increasing their intellectual flexibility and resilience and deriving deep and lasting pleasure and gratification by "diversification" of their interests and pursuits outside their work spheres.

My contacts with large numbers of men and women of almost all ages, backgrounds and occupations have proved many things to me. Among them is the fact that almost any person of reasonable intelligence has the potential capacity to master the fine art of living.

He or she may be 21 or 91 or any age in between. As long as a few simple rules are followed, success is certain.

First, the individual should choose pursuits and pastimes from which he or she derives genuine enjoyment and satisfaction.

Second, whatever one decides to do, it should be done enthusiastically and energetically, with a maximum of personal involvement in the project or activity.

Third, it must always be borne in mind that the conveniences and facilities provided by our affluent era are *not* ends in themselves. They are excellent tools, helpful means for accomplishing desired ends.

Finally, the individual must possess and exercise both the will and the determination to live life to the utmost, and to gain the utmost out of living.

I firmly believe, and have seen ample proof, that in this Age of Affluence, each and every period in the average person's lifetime can be—and should be—a Golden Age. The process that produces the desired results is surprisingly simple.

The elements are all at hand. The individual needs only to select those required by his or her personal formula, combine them in the correct proportions, and mix them with enthusiasm and vigor.

The alchemy is infallible, the transmutation miraculous!

2 HCL—THE HIGH CHANCE OF LONGEVITY

Average life expectancy has increased some 150 percent since the eighteenth century. Astounding strides made by medical science and other factors have literally added decades to the average American's life since 1900, and new discoveries and advances are continuing to add more and more years. Living and working conditions have also been immensely improved. The majority of our population enjoys more boons and benefits than any other human group in history. The question that remains to be answered is how to make a long life a full, fully rewarding—in short, a merry— one.

We all might as well adjust and accustom ourselves to the idea.

HCL is with us—and, what is more, there is every indication it will continue to spiral upward.

No, I am not talking about the High Cost of Living.

I am referring to the High Chance of Longevity—the eminently favorable odds that you who are reading these words will live a long time—on the average, many years or even decades longer than the members of any other human group in history.

Proof?

Of course. But first, let us establish a basis for comparison, or rather, as will become evident, a basis for sharp and striking contrast.

Vide, then, the prideful boast to be found in the *Encyclopedia Britannica* of 1797:

In the eighteenth century, *the probability of life has increased to twenty-seven years and two months; and the mean life to thirty-two years and two months.* (Emphasis added.)

Moving ahead a hundred years or so, and focusing attention on our own country, we can easily discern and trace a trend that makes these "gains" appear pathetic indeed:

- In 1900, the average length of life in the United States was a shade over 47 years.
- By 1930, the figure had risen to almost 60 years.
- In 1966, the average had passed the 70-year mark and was moving steadily higher.

The salutary effects of this soaring HCL index are clearly visible in our present-day population statistics. The United States Census Bureau estimates there are now:

- Approximately 56 million Americans aged 45 and over.
- Of these, about 25 million are 60 or older.
- Among those in the 60-plus age group, nearly *7 million* men and women are over 75.

Incidentally, and as a warming sidelight, the last (1960) census revealed that there were some 14,000 Americans who had reached or exceeded the age of 100. What is more, according to the flurries of newspaper and magazine articles and interviews that followed the Census Bureau's release of the information, not a few of the centenarians were doing quite well, thank you.

(Witness, for somewhat head-spinning example, Judge Albert Alexander of Plattsburg, Missouri. Then a mere 103, His Honor—by apparently reliable reports—"never failed to arrive in court on time"!)

Impressive as they are, the "average length of life" figures and Census Bureau estimates I've cited fail to tell the whole story. The "averages" are for the overall population. They do not indicate how many among us may reasonably expect to live to any given age. Nor do they reflect the average remaining lifetime at various age levels. As for the Census Bureau estimates, they provide little if any indication of probable future trends.

Luckily, this data is available from the "Average Future Lifetime" tables prepared by the Department of Health, Education and Welfare. The paraphrasing of some selected extracts from the tables will convey at a glance the truly bright prospects for long life in our era and society.

For instance:

- Upon reaching your 60th birthday—and about 8 in every 10 Americans will do so—you will have an average remaining lifetime of nearly 18 years.
- When you reach 75—which very close to half our entire population will do—you may, in all probability, look forward to 9 additional years of life.
- As you blow out the candles on your 85th-birthday cake (and, roughly speaking, 1 in every 5 Americans is expected to do precisely that) you will still have an average remaining lifetime of over four and a half years ahead of you!

The phenomenal increases in human life expectancy since the turn of the twentieth century did not "just happen." The miracles were wrought by interlocking and interacting forces and factors, achievements and advances in scientific, social and economic spheres.

Unquestionably, by far the largest share—albeit not all—of the credit belongs to science, and particularly medical science. Numerous diseases which once exterminated thousands each year have virtually ceased to exist. The menace of many others has been markedly reduced. The following comparisons suffice to illustrate the prodigious strides made by medicine since the beginning of the century:

Type of Disease	DEATH RATES (Number per year per 100,000 population)	
	1900	1964
Typhoid & paratyphoid	36.0	——
Tuberculosis	201.9	4.3
Influenza & pneumonia	181.5	31.1

The understanding of and emphasis on such general health principles as personal and public hygiene and sanitation and proper diet (including vitamin requirements) also figure prominently in the record of medicine's contributions to the prolongation of human life over the last several decades.

But, spurred on by the gains already registered, science and scientists are striving harder than ever to achieve the utopian goal of a disease-free civilization. New drugs, improved methods and techniques, fresh discoveries and advances are being reported almost daily. Furthermore, a rapidly growing body of scientific talent throughout the world is concerning itself directly with the mysteries of the aging process, seeking the means by which it may be retarded, halted or even reversed. Some medical authorities confidently declare that a decisive breakthrough in this area, if not yet actually within sight, is just over the near horizon.

One especially sanguine prophet is Dr. Edward M. Henderson, president of the Aging Research Institute. This privately endowed organization has sponsored intensive studies of the aging process by such prestigious institutions as the Columbia University College of Physicians and Surgeons.

"We should be living to the age of 150 now, in our own day," Dr. Henderson has been widely quoted as saying.

It may, I trust, be presumed that the Doctor's statement is not merely wishful thinking but has at least some basis in the data obtained through his organization's research projects.

Dr. Peter Brian Medawar, the Briton who shared the Nobel Prize for Medicine and Physiology in 1960, is another exponent of the burgeoning school of thought that contemptuously rejects Seneca's classic aphorism: "Old age is an incurable disease."

On the contrary, Dr. Medawar and others hold, few if any human beings waste away from age per se. They argue that what we call "old age" is simply a *result* of disease.

The gist of their theory is that the deleterious and destructive effects of disease on a human being's vital organs and processes are the factors determining the length of his or her life span. And, they contend: cure or eliminate the disease or diseases, repair the damage they have done, restore or replace that which has been destroyed, and you vanquish age completely.

Now, I make no pretense of being either scientist or medical authority. I neither conducted scientific researches into the subject under discussion nor studied the findings and reports of those who have. I speak purely as a duly impressed—even awed—layman when I suggest that the past performances of medical science are persuasive enough to lend plausibility to its optimistic forecasts for the future.

On the other hand, as I noted earlier, science cannot take *all* the credit for the increase in human life expectancy. Social, economic and even technological reforms, changes and improvements have also played influential roles by ameliorating the average person's everyday existence and creating more salubrious living and working environments and conditions.

How, for example, could anyone have expected a laborer or clerk and his family to live long—never mind decently—in the late but totally unlamented laissez-faire era of the nineteenth century?

Reflecting the attitudes prevalent in certain quarters during that period are the utterances of the Reverend Henry Ward Beecher. Then a renowned, influential and ostentatiously wealthy public figure, Beecher preached the gospel of abject poverty—for the "working classes." In 1877, he sermonized that "a dollar a day" was an adequate wage for a man with "a wife and five or six children." A dollar, said the Reverend, was "enough to buy bread with. Water costs nothing, and a man who cannot live on bread is not fit to live."

Incredible as it sounds in this day and age, these remarks were widely advertised and applauded!

At the start of the twentieth century, 60-hour (or even longer) workweeks and 15-cent-an-hour (and even lower)

wage scales were hardly uncommon. I myself remember working as a roustabout in the Oklahoma fields in 1909, when I
was still in my teens. The regular workweek consisted of six
12-hour shifts—and I'd rather not think of what I received
as wages.

For that matter, in 1928—a peak, pre-stock-market-crash
"prosperity" year—men employed as weavers in New England
mills worked 48 hours a week for $25; in the southern states,
they worked 55 hours for $18. Women performing identical
tasks worked the same hours and received $21.50 in the New
England region, $16 in the South. And, it should be remarked
in passing, in 1928, weavers—men or women, in the North
or South—were hardly at the very bottom of the labor-force
ladder; many others worked longer hours and earned less.

Even if one makes full allowance for the greater actual
buying power of a dollar in 1900 or 1928, it is still obvious
that the wages paid in the respective years to large numbers
of workers were sufficient to maintain a family only at bare
subsistence levels.

The hours? Well, how would any average individual's physical system react to 60, 72 or more hours of back-breaking
toil each week when his or her diet, clothing and shelter were
all inadequate?

Into the bargain, until comparatively recently, the great
mass of our people had to face and endure unnumbered
hardships and risks that could—and often did—quite literally
eat up their lives.

Factories, mills, offices were frequently poorly heated or
ventilated. Little thought—and less care—were given to proper
lighting, the presence and effects of toxic fumes and substances, safety devices and equipment. Who has not heard of
the 1911 Triangle Shirtwaist fire in New York? More than 140
people—mainly women—died when the factory burned. Management, afraid some of its employees might slip outside for a
few minutes during working hours, habitually locked all the
doors leading to and from workrooms. Thus, when the blaze
started, the workers could not escape!

A sizable segment of our population did not have things
very well "at home," either, a few decades ago. Houses and
apartments workers could afford were seldom adequately

heated, and sanitary facilities were often primitive to the extreme. For housewives, life was, as often as not, sheer, grinding drudgery. Little wonder that so many women "looked old before their time" in the 1900s and, to a somewhat lesser extent, in the 1920s.

But enough of this dismal recital. Let us return to *now*, when most of our population enjoys a considerably happier lot, and a much higher chance of longevity, than ever before.

Today, 40-hour—and, in more than a few occupations and industries, appreciably shorter—workweeks are standard. Wage scales vary, but in 1967 the average hourly pay in manufacturing industries exceeded $2.80 and the national median family income was almost touching $7,436 per year.

Not long ago, temporary layoffs and brief illnesses—let alone protracted unemployment or sickness—spelled disaster, a total loss of income for the average person. Nowadays, almost all people who work receive some compensation for a reasonable period if they lose their jobs or are unable to hold down their jobs due to illness. In the fiscal year 1966–67, the nationwide average of weekly benefits paid to unemployed persons was $41.05—no prodigal bounty in view of current living costs, but surely infinitely better than nothing.

In the 1960s, an employee unable to work as a result of injuries suffered on the job will, most probably, receive disability benefits. Various forms of hospitalization and health insurance provide at least minimal protection for a large, and steadily expanding, segment of our populace. According to the Health Insurance Institute, United States insurance companies covered only 3.7 million people with hospital insurance in 1940. By 1966, they were providing hospital expense protection to a net total of more than 97 million Americans—nearly half the entire population of the country.

Pension and retirement programs, improved housing, industrial safety standards . . .

Public health programs, adequate heating and modern sanitary facilities on the job and in the home . . .

Labor-saving devices for use at work and in the house, balanced diets, more schooling, more leisure time . . .

These are but a random and purposely jumbled sampling of some other items in the bulging mixed bag of benefits most of our citizens enjoy today. All operate to make the average person's existence easier, more comfortable and more secure. They lighten the physical burdens and go far toward dissipating the gnawing fears and uncertainties that were once—and not overly long ago—day-to-day staples for the greatest number. Each of the benefits consequently contributes in some measure to the individual's general health and well-being— and hence ultimately to his or her prospects for living well beyond the traditional "allotted" span of "three-score years and ten."

When all is said and done, we return to the observation I made at the opening of this chapter. HCL—the continually increasing High Chance of Longevity—is a reality of the here and now.

People—and, if I may be permitted a mild and amiable vulgarism, this includes you—simply have to face the fact that they are very likely to be alive for quite a while.

When the fact has been fully comprehended, only one question remains:

How to make a long *life a merry one.*

3 ON DISDAINING MYTHS AND DISCARDING MISCONCEPTIONS

Several glaring fallacies and falsehoods which people for some reason accept as truths and facts serve to inhibit them from enjoying life to the utmost. "Youth" and "age" as qualitative rather than quantitative terms. Some eye-opening examples of men and women who have refused to accept chronological age as a factor limiting or controlling their activities. The myth of the set and inflexible course as a road to success in life. Evidence and argument that it's never too late to change—and that opportunity is very likely to knock often in every person's life.

It was, if memory serves me, Cicero who observed that "Man is his own worst enemy."

Indeed, we humans do sometimes demonstrate a perverse talent for making things more difficult for ourselves. Witness, for immediately pertinent instance, how many people are wont to embrace trite myths and misconceptions that inhibit them from fully realizing their own potentials and prevent them from reaping the rewards life has to offer.

Among the more pernicious of these fictions is one epitomized in a hoary proverb: "If youth but knew, and age were able."

With all due apology to the original author and to those who accept the adage as Universal Truth, I beg to take issue. On the whole, the proverb is a double-barreled fallacy; its implications are valid only in certain narrow areas, and then not always or in all cases.

In the first place, the terms "youth" and "age" are relative —and qualitative rather than quantitative. As we have seen, the human life span has increased enormously; what was "age" in the 1700s—or, for that matter, in 1900—might well be "youth" today. Then, of course, individual characteristics and differences must be taken into account. This, incidentally, was succinctly—and amusingly—emphasized some months ago in a much-quoted statement attributed to film actress Maureen O'Sullivan.

"I know people who are antiques at 35 and others who can Watusi at 70," she said.

Now, personally, I, at 75, still prefer the Twist, but that is neither here nor there. The point is that one person's dotage may easily be another's prime.

Finally—and above all it must be borne in mind that there have always been men and women who "knew"—who possessed mental and emotional balance and mature judgment —in their youth. By the same token, there have always been men and women who, notwithstanding their comparatively advanced chronological age, remained entirely "able"—entirely competent to think and act, achieve and create, direct and lead.

Striking illustrations of the extremes are provided by two men generally conceded to rank among history's greatest statesmen: British Prime Ministers William Pitt the Younger and Sir Winston Churchill. Pitt assumed office when he was only 24. Sir Winston served as Prime Minister twice—first from his sixty-sixth to seventy-first and again from his seventy-sixth to eighty-first years. Viewing their records of achievement, it would be absurd to suggest that the "stripling" Pitt did not "know" or that the "venerable" Churchill was not "able."

However, evidence to pulverize the proverb into the dust

of fable was never lacking and has certainly become over-whelming in recent times.

I assume that everyone is well aware of how high the "know quotient" of "youth" has climbed in the twentieth century. For decades there have been scientists and scholars, engineers and entrepreneurs, painters and politicians—men and women in every field—who, though still in their twenties or very early thirties, proved themselves eminently qualified and achieved notable success. After all, this is the era in which we even have a Young Presidents Organization for individuals who become heads of companies grossing a million dollars or more a year *before* they reach 40.

For some unfathomable reason it is less widely recognized that, while youth has been proving it "knows," age has been proving it is remarkably "able." But a quick, kaleidoscopic sampling of well-known examples offers eloquent testimony to the fact.

Rhode Island Senator Theodore Green was ranked among the nation's outstanding and most respected solons—from when he was first elected at 69 until he stepped down from office at 93.

- Alfred P. Sloan, Jr., was 89 in 1964, when he published his book *My Years with General Motors*, which stayed on the best-seller lists for 22 weeks.
- In 1966, divorcée Marion "Molly" Hart, 74, flew solo across the Atlantic in a single-engine aircraft.
- Mrs. Alice Roosevelt Longworth, daughter of President Theodore Roosevelt, reached 83 in 1967. According to published reports, she regularly read until dawn, gave two or three dinner parties each week and attended countless Washington social affairs.
- Lieutenant General Lewis Hershey, 74 in 1967, remained active head of the United States Selective Service System.
- Former union chief John L. Lewis, despite his 86-plus years, has been reported to appear daily at his office and with a sharp eye oversee United Mine Workers pension and welfare funds.
- At the University of Kentucky, some 160 students, rang-

ing in age from the late 60s to almost 80, have "gone back to college." They are studying practically everything, from modern dancing and creative writing to science and foreign languages—and having the time of their lives.

● The International Executive Service Corps, composed mainly of retired business executives, is doing yeoman work providing technical and managerial advice and assistance to privately owned companies all over the globe. This "Paunch Corps," as it has been good-naturedly nicknamed by its members, has been called "a priceless asset" of the United States economic aid program.

While whole volumes could be devoted to such myth-defying examples as these, it remains for each individual to realize for himself or herself that there is no valid reason to be abashed by one's youth or afraid of one's age.

"I may be 84, but that doesn't alter the basic facts of time and of living one iota," a particularly active and contented octogenarian told me recently.

Somewhat baffled by the remark, I asked him to elaborate.

"It's really very simple," he chuckled. "When I was 21, there were 1,440 minutes in a day, 7 days in a week and 52 weeks in a year. The figures have remained the same—and so has my outlook. I've always tried to get all I could out of every minute, day, week and year—and I still do."

Therein, it seems to me, lies a fundamental ingredient of the formula for demolishing the "If youth but knew, and age were able" fiction, for beginning a productive, gratifying life early and continuing to live it for an extraordinary period.

"Set your course and stick to it, no matter what happens," is the gist of another familiar sophistry that some people accept literally and as an axiom, thus building obstacles to hinder their progress and pleasure in life. Laudable as it may seem on the surface, this "press on regardless" philosophy can be tantamount to placing an individual's feet firmly, irrevocably and forever into a groove that usually leads to a dead end.

Yes, of course, it is wise to set goals and plan the courses for attaining them. On the other hand, it is essential to remain flexible and adaptable so that one can readily adjust and adapt to changing conditions, meet unforseen contingencies and take advantage of new opportunities.

During my career as a wildcatting operator, I learned numberless important lessons in the manifestly practical, frill-free school of the oil field. I have long since discovered that the majority of them are applicable—at least by analogy —to almost all aspects of life and everyday living.

For example, whenever I spudded a well, it was my "goal" to strike oil, to bring in a producing well. Nevertheless, there were occasions—more of them than I'd care to count or remember—when, after the drilling bit reached a certain depth, it became evident no oil was to be found on the site. Once established, the unpalatable truth had to be faced and swallowed whole. To have continued drilling—to have "stuck" to the "set course"—would have meant throwing good time, effort, energy and money after bad. There was no choice but to abandon course and goal—and the dry hole—and start afresh elsewhere.

"To get along in this business, you've got to know when to stand pat, and when to zig or zag or back down," a grizzled veteran wildcatter once advised me.

The counsel applies to any "business" and to every sphere of human existence. It is infinitely sounder advice than any that holds one must never, under whatever circumstances, revise—or, heaven forbid, discard—previously established goals, plans or programs. Determination, persistence and tenacity are splendid qualities—provided they are tempered by reason, common sense and the capacity to assess and evaluate people and situations. Otherwise they add up to a negative sum of blind and futile obstinacy.

It is no rare event for an individual to find himself in a situation or position where changes—or even major upheavals —are indicated. If, after weighing all the pertinent factors and elements and determining that the changes will be advantageous or worthwhile, the individual still permits himself to be bound by the straitjacket of the "stick to it" myth, he is liable to long rue and regret his failure to "zig" or "zag."

In the opening months of 1942, I found myself in precisely such a quandary. World War II had begun, and I could have gone on as before, devoting my time and efforts to my oil business. But Navy Secretary Frank Knox informed me that the then tiny Spartan Aircraft Corporation—a subsidiary of a company in which I held a sizable interest—could make an important contribution to the nation's war effort provided its facilities and operations were greatly expanded.

I knew little about manufacturing, less about aircraft production—and I was nearing 50. Nonetheless, after a brief debate with myself, I dropped everything else and took over active management of Spartan "for the duration." Seldom if ever in my life and career have I derived greater satisfaction than I did from personally nurturing the company and seeing it burgeon into a major "defense plant" that produced great quantities of war material for our own and Allied air forces.

There are innumerable far more impressive stories. Some were related a short while ago in a *Time* magazine article on "career switchers"—people who, despite having achieved success in their jobs and professions, felt themselves to be in a rut and decided to take drastic measures and satisfy their innermost longings and desires.

Among the remarkable case histories cited by *Time* were these:

- Gilbert Daniels, sales manager for a computer company, quit his job at 38, obtained a Ph.D. in botany—and, although his future income will be less than his previous *income tax*, is now immeasurably happier and more content than before.
- Mrs. Carolyn Sadow, a successful advertising executive at 50, resigned her position, went back to college and has realized her long-repressed desire to be a library specialist.
- Sixty-year-old Herbert Summers, feeling frustrated as a mechanical and civil engineer, obtained a master's degree in oceanographic geology and is now a pleased-as-punch scuba-diving scientist.

In short, regardless of their profession, position, age or other considerations, people can—and do—drastically alter their plans and make major changes in their lives and living and working patterns. And, very often, they gain more from life and experience greater gratification because they temporarily shelve or permanently discard old objectives and set entirely new and different goals for themselves.

A prominent mark of all successful leaders—political, military, business or whatever—is their ability to plan wisely and well. But the greatest among them are invariably those who, when it is necessary or advisable, can quickly and effectively amend plans, shift short-range tactics or revise long-range strategy. In these respects, the average person will clearly benefit by playing follow-the-leader, by emulating those whose achievements prove the reliability of their methods.

The foregoing arguments and examples that explode the "never—but *never*—alter your course" myth also help destroy a related and somewhat overlapping misconception: that one should always choose the safest path and, whatever the cost or consequence, avoid all risks.

Methinks that devotees of this dubious doctrine are merely showing they would rather be vegetables than individuals. They fail to recognize—or do not care—that Absolute Security is but a short step from Absolute Stultification.

Safety first?

Yes, of course.

But safety first, last and always?

One might as well spend life locked inside a bank vault, a dungeon or a tomb.

Please do not misunderstand me. I definitely am *not* recommending that anyone take unnecessary or unjustified risks —be they physical, financial or otherwise. However, for a human being to remain a vital entity and for the human mind to remain active and alert, there must be some element of challenge, some spirit of adventure in existence. Only thus may an individual satisfy the innate human need for experiencing a sense of triumph at having accomplished anything. Only thus can he say to himself: "I have managed to overcome odds and obstacles, and I have won!"

There is no zest, exhilaration or real satisfaction in a cut-and-dried, insulated, amniotic and armor-plated existence. Like unseasoned *ersatz* food—which may sustain life but provides scant pleasure or enjoyment to whoever eats it—super-safety offers nothing for the intellect or emotions to savor.

"If there weren't so many risks involved, I'd go into business for myself tomorrow."

"We'd buy the beautiful house we looked at last week—only we're afraid real estate values might drop."

"My wife and I want children, but . . ."

"It's long been my desire to move out to the West Coast—and I would, except that I'm worried about all the uncertainties involved."

Broadly speaking, be it in wooing fair maiden, bearding irascible boss or any other effort to obtain one's desires or better one's lot, there is always a certain element of risk present. And, more often than not, the potential rewards are proportionate to the degree of calculated risks taken in the striving for them. Timid ifs, onlys, buts and excepts are the brick walls against which the happiness and gratification are soon battered out of life and living. The individual who avoids all challenge and risk is not showing cowardice nearly as much as he is confessing impotence and condemning himself to a life of joyless mediocrity.

Yet another—and, if gullibly accepted, insurmountable—bar to a full life is the colossal *bêtise* that opportunity knocks but once. It never ceases to amaze me how many people actually believe this patent absurdity and are convinced that, having missed one boat somewhere along the line, they are permanently stranded without hope of ever again finding transportation anywhere.

Opportunity does not limit itself to one knock per lifetime. People are constantly being presented with opportunities; they need only to recognize and seize them. Miss some—and we all do on occasion—and while the schedules tend to be irregular, other boats will be along sooner or later. On the other hand, although the later vessels have the same destinations as the first, they often charge higher fares—as is conspicuously evidenced by two of my own experiences.

In 1932, I could have obtained a valuable oil concession in the Middle East for a small—practically negligible—sum, but I failed to take advantage of the opportunity. My second chance did not arrive until 1948–49, when a concession became available in the Neutral Zone on the Persian Gulf. I did not allow it to slip out of my hands—but the price had soared astronomically over the intervening years. Opportunity's second knock cost an immediate cash payment of $12.5 million!

In 1950, my friend the Duke of Argyll invited me to visit his ancestral castle, where, he told me, he had "some pieces of eighteenth-century French furniture" he desired to sell. It was winter, and I balked at taking a trip to northern Scotland in the cold weather—and I thereby lost the first opportunity to add a superb example of eighteenth-century furniture to my collection. Not until a year or so later did I learn that one of the pieces was the magnificent "Husband and Wife Desk" produced by the master craftsman "BvRB" (identified by experts as Bernard van Riesenberg). By then, the desk had passed through several hands and was owned by a New York dealer. Yes, I purchased it—at a figure doubtless much higher than I would have paid if I'd accepted the Duke's invitation and bought it from him directly.

Withal, the truly enterprising individual refuses to wait for opportunity to knock again; he will create his own. A dramatic, inspiring example is to be found in the widely publicized story of an indomitable Kentuckian, Harland Sanders. Less than fifteen years ago, Sanders owned a large, thriving restaurant that specialized in southern fried chicken. Then the rerouting of a highway wrecked the restaurant's business and threw Harland Sanders into bankruptcy. In 1955, he was 65—and living on the "old age" benefits he received from the Social Security Administration.

Undaunted by his bad fortune and unmindful of his years, Sanders became a traveling salesman, going from state to state selling his private and unique recipe for making fried chicken. From these less-than-modest (and even less auspicious) beginnings, he built the Kentucky Fried Chicken Corporation, which, according to *Newsweek* magazine, is today "one of the largest food franchise operations in the world with 1,115 outlets deployed in the U.S. and around the globe." *Newsweek* added that Sanders, 76 when the story on him appeared in July, 1966, was a millionaire and still hard at work, creating more new opportunities for himself.

Last, but not least, among the more familiar misconceptions that I believe operate to diminish painfully the rewards and joys of life is "tunnel vision"—inordinate emphasis on "singleness of purpose." The individual, fixing his attention on a single pinpoint objective, sets off in hot pursuit of it, completely blind and indifferent to all else around him.

A person who has but a sole aim and whose interests are otherwise narrowly restricted or nonexistent soon grows dull, stale and ineffectual. He or she acquires no depth of understanding or breadth of experience and eventually learns the goal is unattainable, for the path leading to it has turned into a one-dimensional treadmill.

Not many months before these words were written, I attended a charity ball in London. At about 3 A.M., in the course of general conversation with the several people at my table, I happened to mention that I'd spent the previous afternoon visiting the Tate Gallery. This prompted a young lady to stare at me with a slightly puzzled expression and ask a question.

"How on earth can you manage all your business affairs and still spend afternoons in art galleries and attend parties like this one?" she inquired.

"It's really quite easy," I replied in all honesty. "In fact, I doubt if I could manage my business affairs properly if I didn't visit galleries, attend parties and do a great many other different things besides."

My point, of course, was that if I concentrated on business to the exclusion of all else, I would soon lose my sense of perspective and proportion. I would atrophy and lose whatever capacity I possessed to decide and direct.

I return to what I said in an earlier chapter about the privileged elite among our eighteenth-century ancestors. They recognized that, to achieve fulfillment and gratification in life, a human being needs to have broad horizons and diversified interests, activities and enthusiasms. And, I reiterate, in our present era and society, these ideals are within reach of the majority, not merely a select few.

A one-track existence is at very best a deadly bore, but it is much more likely to prove an express route to the limbo of extinguished egos and immolated ids.

These, then, are some of the more ubiquitous myths and misconceptions which, I have observed, are major obstacles to the enjoyment of life and living. It has been my intention to examine—and my hope to demolish—them.

I'm afraid it's highly probable that people who insist on or persist in believing the fictions and fallacies go far toward defeating themselves from the very beginning. Each day is likely to prove a source of added frustration and disappointment, causing them to rue and resent their existence.

But individuals who reject or discard the myths establish a firm and promising foundation on which to build their futures. They not only rid themselves of enormous handicaps, but they take a large and important initial step along the road to a full, happy and thoroughly gratifying existence. Free of the inhibiting influence of humbug, having the advantage of a head start, they should be able to take the succeeding steps, calmly and confidently.

4   FOR BETTER BEGINNINGS

The person who faces certain facts from the start helps ensure that his or her life will be easier, better and more gratifying. It's often necessary to make compromises, allowances and adjustments —but this does not mean the individual must sacrifice his hopes or ambitions or destroy his individuality. Almost everyone lives in two separate—but overlapping—spheres of existence; the wise person seeks to achieve harmony between both. And, to establish a sound basis, it is essential to separate the wheat of the possible from the chaff of the impossible; much of the task can be done by answering six simple questions.

Unfortunately, even after the major initial obstacles and barriers have been removed from the starting line, the route to a full and happy life is still not a glassy-smooth superhighway. It still has its detours, blind curves, crossroads, toll stations and, especially, its regulatory restrictions.

Precious few individuals—be they philosophers or fools, magnates or mendicants—are free to traverse the thoroughfare as they please. At least, not as long as they encounter other traffic along the road and find it necessary to coexist and interact with other human beings.

True, here as ever there are some exceptions to the rule that people must obey rules. One *can* take a cutoff to some

remote mountain fastness and there enjoy "total freedom"—
but only at a Stone Age level and only as long as one remains
completely isolated and self-sufficient. For at the moment the
anchorite needs to obtain so much as a crust, a scrap of cloth
or a nail from another human being, he automatically surren-
ders a degree of his freedom by making himself subject to
terms and conditions set by another person or by society as a
whole.

Since there are not many among us harboring cravings for
a diet of roots and berries, a wardrobe of primitively cured
animal pelts or an abode in a cave, it remains for the over-
whelming majority to acknowledge and respect the regulations, rules and realities of civilization. In order to qualify as
functioning members of our society, people therefore need to
tolerate certain encroachments on their individual liberties
by that society. Failure to do so results in penalties being
exacted.

For instance, a citizen is forbidden—under pain of punishment—to commit burglary or bigamy, cheat or choke his
neighbor, fight a duel or forge a deed. And, for that matter,
the average citizen is not even allowed absolute discretion in
disposing of his own personal earnings; appreciable portions
of these are automatically deducted by, or must be handed
over to, an array of tax authorities.

Yes, certainly these and similar restrictions and regulations
are intended to protect the safety and welfare of the citizenry
and protect and preserve our social system and fabric. Nonetheless, in pure theory if naught else, there *are* infringements
on the concept of Absolute Individual Freedom.

In all fairness, it must be admitted that the average person
is aware of such circumscriptions and by and large submits
to and abides by them without undue protest. But, paradoxically, he conforms even more voluntarily to many other less
conspicuous, more sweeping and decisive limitations which
are imposed on us all, even though their very existence—to
say nothing of their operative effects—are consciously recognized by only an insignificant minority.

As an example, while the average American enjoys great
freedom of choice and decision in most areas of his activity,
he is by no means an entirely free agent when it comes to

setting the course of his life. He is subject to a profusion of forces, factors and circumstances to which he must react and respond. And he barely, if at all, realizes that they obtain and operate, even though they frequently impel or compel his more important decisions and actions.

Those who might consider this debatable had best begin by recognizing that, in the course of their lifetimes, it is necessary for them to make many greater or lesser allowances and adjustments, compromises and concessions merely to survive and even more if they hope to rise above the faceless mass. Often, when confronted with a choice of options, they are forced to forego what would normally be their first selection and settle for, or on, alternatives or mediums—and only then may they proceed to make the most of them.

I know this all too well from my experience. As a youth, it was my ambition and desire to enter the United States Diplomatic Service and—when, as and if my career therein permitted—engage in a secondary vocation as a writer. I probably would have done so, too, had it not been for the seeming irrelevancy that I was an only child.

This made all—the decisive—difference. Someone would have to carry on the business my father, George F. Getty, had built up over many decades of hard and dedicated work. It wasn't that I was the best-suited or even logical candidate; it just so happened that I was the only one available.

I assure you, the idea of managing a fair-size and successful business was not only a far cry from my original ambitions, but a formidable and perturbing prospect. The attendant responsibilities and problems loomed large, heavy and ominously burdensome. But there were no emergency exits through which I could in good conscience evade them, particularly since my mother's security and welfare were also involved and at stake.

Consequently, I abandoned my cherished plans and made my career in the business world rather than in the Diplomatic Service. Once my decision was made, I allowed myself no masochistic luxuries of lingering regrets. I could ill have afforded them in view of the tasks that had to be undertaken.

Admittedly, the "game" was not my first choice, but one into which I had been sent as a substitute player by circumstances over which I had scant control. Nevertheless—and regardless of how I got there—I *was* in the game, and the starting whistle had blown. From then on, it behooved me to participate in it energetically and actively, and keep the ball in play.

Lest there be any misunderstandings, I hasten to disavow any intention of boasting or making claim to any virtues. I am merely using myself as a convenient example to support two contentions. First, that while an individual cannot always have or do what he wants most, he can nonetheless and assuredly adjust and acclimate himself to a reasonable alternative or rational medium. Second, he can still derive pleasure and satisfaction from his occupation and enjoyment from life and living.

Experience has shown me there is nothing more futile or senseless than to waste energy bemoaning and fulminating against the necessity for making compromises and concessions in life. One might just as well rant and rave against the laws prohibiting mayhem and murder because a weather forecaster wrongly predicted clear skies and a sudden cloudburst ruined a family picnic.

After all, seldom does an individual's acceptance of the inevitable equate with abject and unconditional surrender. Nor does it necessarily imply that he must thenceforth renounce his deep-seated aspirations and ambitions and condemn himself to utter despondency.

On the one hand, imaginative and resourceful individuals will broaden the base and structure of their situations to provide ample room and opportunity for realizing their ambitions and fulfilling their desires within the expanded framework. On the other—as we saw in the immediately preceding chapter—it's never "too late" for courageous and enterprising men and women to raise themselves out of what they consider ruts and switch to entirely different careers or develop new interests which will satisfy their innermost longings.

However, and in all events, it must be a foremost consideration that, for much of his adult lifetime, the average individual will move in two distinct, yet overlapping and interrelated, spheres of existence: the "vocational" (that which involves his work) and the personal. And, for good, bad or indifferent, any vocational or career situation is bound to exert significant and more or less formative pressures on an individual's overall life philosophy and living patterns.

A person who learns or absorbs nothing from, and remains blindly impervious to, an environment in which he or she spends forty or so hours each week is rare enough to be unique. It is extremely improbable that anyone can blot his or her "job" completely from mind upon leaving the office or passing through the factory gates. Practically everyone "talks shop" away from work; this alone would appear to prove that thoughts and impressions are "carried home." Whether these occupational influences are visibly prepotent or deceptively subtle depends on unnumbered factors, but they do unquestionably have their effects, and I rely on the glaringly simple and obvious for illustration.

An airline pilot flying the transatlantic run and an upper-bracket buyer for a department store are likely to receive comparable incomes, but it isn't very likely their philosophies and private lives will be similar. The night-shift machinist and midnight-to-dawn disc jockey both work odd hours, but each develops his own thinking and living patterns, and these, in turn, will have little resemblance to those of the corner druggist or local supermarket manager. A private secretary and a registered nurse are both women, and presumably both have similar basic feminine instincts and qualities, but I'm inclined to queston if their viewponts and perspectives—and their life patterns—will be anywhere near identical.

And, in my opinion, a goodly portion of these differences may be reasonably ascribed to the influences of work situations and experiences.

All things considered, I think most of us will, if we are honest about it, concede that human beings are not really as much the masters of their destinies and captains of their fate as it pleases them to believe. Yet no one can deny that, within the limits imposed on them, they possess more than adequate freedom and latitude to make what they will—and are able to make—of themselves, their lives and their careers.

Some, it is deplorable but true, will make nothing, advance nowhere and be abject failures in either or both—and usually both—spheres of their existence solely because they refuse to make the requisite effort to do more or better. For these individuals, the rest of us need spare scarcely more than a casual glance, or, if we are so inclined, a glum shake of the head.

Others may make an honest and forceful effort but will fail due to intellectual or other shortcomings or even physical infirmities. These individuals are certainly deserving of understanding, sympathy and, where indicated and justified, a helping hand.

Yet others will achieve success—greater or lesser, depending no less on their own scales of measurement than on their abilities—in one or both spheres (and one hopes for their sake it will be in both). While they are often aided in some measure by others or by that indefinable element called "luck," their successes will still be due in large part to their own talents, efforts and exertions.

However, it strikes me that before any individual begins striving in all-out earnest to attain his aspirations in life and work, he is entitled to receive a few words of rather unconventional caution.

Basing my opinion on years of observation and experience, I have come to the conclusion that almost as many individuals fail because they try to do too much as fail because they do not do enough.

Yes, I know. This sounds paradoxical and smacks of heresy. But, unfortunately, it is true of numerous people. Their basic weakness can be described very briefly. In whichever—or both —spheres of their existence, "vocational" or personal, they seek to achieve and accomplish, they are simply incapable of determining what is possible, within their capacity to reach, and what is impossible, or beyond their grasp, no matter how far they stretch.

They set their sights too high, and then, to their disappointment, see that their most carefully aimed shots have missed the mark.

All this reminds me of an executive—let us charitably call him by the fictitious name John Jones—who once, rather briefly, worked for one of the companies I control. Intelligent, well educated, with a very pleasant personality, a lovely family and a good record in lesser executive jobs with other firms, he appeared suited for the responsible position to which he was appointed.

The honeymoon was short-lived. It wasn't long before it became apparent that John Jones was not only failing to move forward, but was falling farther and farther behind, dragging other company executives with him. The entire organization was floundering helplessly in a tidal wave of backlogged work, delayed projects and customers' furious complaints.

It did not require much searching to locate the trouble. Either friend Jones's new job had gone to his head or he was trying desperately to prove himself—with the net result that he lost all sense of proportion. He believed that he—and the organization he managed—could work miracles, do anything and everything in a preposterously short time. Whatever anyone wanted or asked, he unhesitatingly promised—if not for tomorrow, then by the day following, without fail. And so, harried and overtaxed personnel were fighting a losing battle against the impossible.

Now, although I am basically a businessman and business considerations should come first, I imagine I might have kept John Jones on the payroll—after shifting him to a less responsible job. He was in his mid-fifties, and I surmised that, with proper handling, he could still do a good job in some lower executive bracket.

I discarded all such notions quickly when it was revealed that Jones had not only badly fumbled in his vocational sphere, but had also made a thorough muddle of his personal life. He'd purchased a house that cost at least twice what his income would justify—with only a minimum down payment. He had been politely, but firmly, asked to resign from the country club to which he belonged after a series of nasty incidents. He was even deeper in debt than he was in uncompleted work and, quiet inquiry disclosed, Jones was a tyrant and terror to his wife and children. John Jones's resignation was demanded—and accepted even before his inked signature was dry.

If anything sets this sad and sorry saga apart from its countless counterparts in all fields, it is the contradiction of seasoning reduce the chances of such near-catastrophic errors.

Having passed the 50 mark, Jones was mature enough, I would say. He'd gone through the mills of both home life and business life. Married for 22 years, he had 3 children: 19, 16 and 14. His past employment record was spotless, reflecting a steady if not spectacular climb. These experiences should have produced a thoroughly seasoned person and business executive. I suppose there is no entirely satisfactory explanation except that he came, he saw—and he was conquered by his own weaknesses.

But never fear, there are plenty of other John Joneses about, and if they serve any constructive purpose, it is as unmistakable stop-look-and-listen warnings to individuals who desire to enjoy life and get ahead in their work.

Anyone aspiring to succeed in the personal and vocational spheres of existence must constantly weigh, measure, gauge and evaluate to determine what can—and cannot—be accomplished under the circumstances that prevail and the resources that are available. In brief, it is essential to separate the wheat of the possible from the chaff of the impossible in both spheres.

The ability to distinguish the frequently extremely fine line that divides the realm of the possible from that of the impossible is rarely an innate trait. It is acquired partially by a process of trial and error, but mainly—or so one hopes—through development of the powers of reasoning and judgment. However, the following questions might help some as jumping-off points for thought and consideration.

- What am I trying to accomplish?
- Why do I think what I want to do is possible?
- What causes me to think it might be impossible?
- What do I stand to gain—or to lose?
- Will such factors as my age, stamina or health have any bearing on the outcome—and, conversely, can I suffer any adverse physical effects by battling the idea (or project or whatever) through?
- Could I utilize my time, efforts and energies to better advantage in other directions?

These, of course, are only suggestions, offered as potential brain stimulators. The final decision rests with the individual involved.

Apropos of the various matters I've covered in this chapter, I would like to relate what I regard as a uniquely appropriate and illuminating anecdote.

Some years ago, I was the dinner guest of a man renowned for his broad intellectual and cultural interests and pursuits, boundless energy, *joie de vivre* and financial success. He was then 75, but looked twenty years younger, swam and took long walks daily and positively abhorred the thought of ever going to bed before 2 A.M.

After dinner, he—and we who were his guests—went into the drawing room. Among those present was a syndicated newspaper columnist unabashedly eager to combine business with pleasure and obtain "human interest" material for one of his articles. He began chatting with our host, politely complimenting him on his notable accomplishments, high honors and astonishing vigor, and then deftly transformed the conversation into an interview.

"Sir, you've achieved so many successes, press and public call you a genius. Do you consider yourself to be one?" the journalist asked.

"Good Lord, no!" was the laughing—and indubitably sincere—reply. "That is, not unless the fact that I long ago recognized some fundamental truths—which, by the way, are available to everyone—constitutes 'genius.' "

"And exactly what are those 'fundamental truths'?" came the next—and predictable—question.

The answer was straightforward, good-natured and, probably because we'd all finished eating only a few minutes earlier, couched in gastronomically oriented figures of speech.

"I'd say there are four. First, a person isn't always able to find every dish he wants on the menu. Second, he can nonetheless usually find enough of a variety to satisfy both his hunger and his palate. Third, while eating, he should obey the old axiom and never bite off more than he can chew. Fourth, this, however, should not prevent him from taking healthy mouthfuls—for any food worth eating should be *eaten,* not toyed with or nibbled in a finicky fashion."

To my way of thinking, these alimentary metaphors deserve

to be committed to memory. At some crucial moment, each will prove to be an invaluable guideline for life and living.

All of them have done so for me.

Many times.

5   MUCH IS IN MIND

Human mind and human will are capable of overcoming many obstacles. An individual's mental attitude toward this, that or another problem or situation may well prove to be the element that makes the difference between success and failure. This is especially true in regard to how a person faces up to the realities of middle age. Some people resign themselves to the idea of becoming "obsolete" as they grow older, while others handily retain their vigor and mental elasticity far beyond the apocryphal "norms" and "limits" set by popular superstition. The examples and lessons are provided by the remarkable Mr. Holmes and several others.

They say life begins at 40. Well, I've reached it, and I know better. It's really the beginning of the end."

"I'm 50. There isn't much of a future left for me."

"Within a month, I'll be 60, and then it'll be the discard pile for me."

These familiar dirges—with occasional variations on their basic theme—are chanted en masse by millions, without much rhyme or reason, but with what amounts to a lemming-like drive for psychological self-destruction.

It does not stand to reason that any normal person would consciously or actively desire to surrender prematurely the satisfactions and pleasures offered by human existence, especially not in our affluent, exciting era and society. But this, in effect, is what incomprehensibly large numbers of people do —or, more precisely, do to themselves.

Don't misunderstand me. I consider flat, unqualified preachments that "age is *all* in the mind" to be specious sops worn threadbare by constant repetition. Yet there are some very large grains of truth to be found beneath the Everests of casuistry and claptrap that have been heaped atop them. An individual's intellectual and emotional preparation, the attitudes he forms vis-à-vis life in general and the passage of years in particular are certainly paramount factors in determining to what extent—and for how long—his existence will be fruitful and gratifying.

Anthropologists have reported cases among aboriginal tribes in which men and women literally willed themselves to death. In our highly civilized society, doctors are frequently known to say, when a patient reaches a critical stage in an illness: "It now depends on whether or not he has the will to live. If he'll fight, he'll make it."

Science—not superstition—has proved that human beings can convince themselves they are suffering from nonexistent sicknesses. The psychosomatic symptom, the hypochondriac and the placebo are as familiar to the physician as tonsilitis, pregnancy or aspirin. If it is within an individual's power to "think" himself into backaches, dizzy spells, ulcers or other debilities, only a bit more effort will be required for him to will himself into decrepitude and senescence at almost any time.

Common experience—not cabalism or esoterics—has proved that human beings can adopt attitudes and outlooks which will keep them "young" intellectually. That done, they can establish patterns and follow regimens which will preserve their "youth"—their vigor and vitality—well past what are widely accepted as being definitive milestones in life.

It's not *all* in the mind—not by a long shot. However, it must start there. As with almost all things, the individual has to begin with his brain and then "follow through."

A prizefighter who climbs into the ring convinced that he has no chance of winning against his adversary has half lost the bout before the gong sounds for the opening of the first round.

A salesman who is overly apprehensive that he will not be able to sell anything to a prospective customer has only a microscopic hope of obtaining an order.

A person who makes up his mind that he cannot possibly learn how to drive a car even before taking a single lesson is not very likely to learn.

I reiterate that I do not subscribe to any far-out theories that mind can always prevail over matter or even over other minds. However, it remains that the less one is hampered and hobbled by mental hazards, the better are his possibilities for achieving his aims. Obviously, the coolly confident and self-possessed boxer, salesman and student driver will have far greater chances of being successful in their endeavors than will their fear-racked, defeatist counterparts.

People, it has been remarked, are roughly divisible into two categories. The first—and, sad to say, large—segment includes those who early resign themselves to what they seem to believe is the inevitability of becoming obsolete, worn out at some given chronological age simply by virtue of reaching that age. Their negativism casts a depressing and repressive pall on their entire existence. They defraud and deprive themselves of much—if not most—of the joys and satisfactions and rewards that should and could rightfully be theirs.

Then there are those individuals who just as early decide to disregard the arbitrary and traditional, to scoff at the preconceived and prejudicial notions of others and, instead, to proceed cheerfully along their own way. They retain throughout their elasticity of mind and exuberance of spirit, remaining "young" in the most remunerative sense of the word. For them, the accretion of years is no tragedy, but rather a perpetually growing fund of experience and experiences which pay a high interest rate and also rich and varied extra dividends.

Now, since it is mainly a matter of personal choice and determination into which category an individual fits in life, it never ceases to mystify me why so many opt for membership in the first group. Whatever reasons there may be for this dismal phenomenon, neither are they rational nor do they reflect much credit on the common sense and imagination of the persons concerned. The "reasons" can indicate only a serious deficiency of mental discipline, will power and tenacity.

Not metaphysics but mundane facts and everyday proofs support the argument that an individual can steer himself into decline or total obsolescence at 40, 50, 60—or at any age, for that matter. And similar considerations support the converse: that a human being can just as easily cause himself to remain at a vital and productive peak far beyond apocryphal "norms" or "limits."

"As to *giving up* because the almanac or the Family Bible says that it is about time to do it, I have no intention of doing any such thing," the senior Oliver Wendell Holmes once wrote —and the emphasis is his.

Therein is expressed the defiant determination that adds active, productive and rewarding years—and even decades— to one's lifetime.

But Holmes was not a man to make a provocative statement and simply let it go at that. "For the encouragement of such as need it," he offered three "treatments" he found effective in combating what some people consider the "malady" of age.

First. As I feel that, when I have anything to do, there is less time for it than when I was younger, I find that I give my attention more thoroughly and use my time more economically than ever before, so that I can learn anything twice as easily as in my earlier days. I am not, therefore, afraid to attack a new study. . . .

Secondly. I have opened my eyes to a good many neglected privileges and pleasures within my reach and requiring only a little courage to enjoy them. . . .

Thirdly. I have found that some of those active exercises which are commonly thought to belong to young folks only may be enjoyed at a much later period.

Holmes declared that he derived great encouragement from "the stories of men who found new occupations when growing old or kept up their common pursuits in the extreme period of life."

After citing such classic examples as those of Cato, who "learned Greek when he was old" and Solon, who "learned something new every day in his old age as he gloried to proclaim," Holmes goes on to recount a tale which I believe bears repetition here.

There is a New England story I have heard more to the point. . . . A young farmer was urged to set out some apple-trees. "No," said he, "they are too long growing and I don't want to plant for other people." The young farmer's father was spoken to about it, but he, with better reason, alleged that apple-trees were slow and life was fleeting. At last, someone mentioned it to the grandfather of the young farmer. He had nothing else to do—so he stuck in some trees. He lived long enough to drink barrels of cider made from the apples that grew on those trees.

The morals are all plain enough. And Oliver Wendell Holmes was as well qualified as anyone to make observations and draw conclusions about human potentials and capabilities.

An example of versatility, he was originally a physician, later a professor of anatomy at Dartmouth and Harvard Medical School (incidentally, he recognized the contagiousness of puerperal fever at the same time as Semmelweis), and then became one of America's foremost men of letters, with few peers as author, essayist, poet and philosopher. Furthermore, his own life was a refutation of statistical probability (born in 1809, he lived to be 85) and of the "if age were able" myth (at 76 he published a major work, the biography of Ralph Waldo Emerson, and continued to write long after that).

Also, it might be noted that he evidently passed his philosophy and durability on to his son and namesake, the eminent jurist Oliver Wendell Holmes, Jr., who was a renowned United States Supreme Court Justice for thirty years—from 1902 until 1932, or three years before his death at ninety-four!

Unfortunately, there are not many of us who are blessed with such outstanding talents and abilities. Nevertheless, there is no earthly reason why we cannot all benefit from the sound counsel and philosophy of the senior Holmes. All of us, at our own respective level of endowment and capacity and within our respective frame of reference, possess the potential to generate a comparable desire and zest for long, constructive life and living.

Holmes compared the human body to a furnace, commenting that "when the fire slackens, life declines." Far too many people seem to have the mistaken idea that by stoking the fire, one burns out the furnace. I am by no means alone in the belief that the opposite is true. If the flames are kept high to provide energy for useful purposes, the furnace will function at optimum efficiency much longer than if the fire is banked or left to smolder.

James A. "Big Jim" Farley celebrated his 79th birthday in 1967. The former political figure and onetime Postmaster General, a 6 foot 3 inch, 205-pound "furnace," was still working a 78-hour week as the export manager of a large soft-drink manufacturing concern. During his seventy-seventh year, he traveled more than 60,000 miles, visiting over a score of countries, attended some 200 official or semiofficial dinners and luncheons—and, even so, managed to keep up with his many other interests and activities.

"The world is a great big wonderful place in which to live," was Farley's smiling comment on his birthday. And, he indicated, there would be no slackening in his active, energetic life.

American-born Sir Alfred Chester Beatty passed the 90 mark, but there was no banking of the fires of his enthusiasm for collecting rare books and manuscripts. His collection, by the way, is acknowledged to be one of the finest of its kind anywhere in the world.

At 75, I frequently find it necessary to work a 16- or even 18-hour day, but as long as I see positive results this neither dismays me nor does it deter me from keeping my personal thermostat set high.

Immobilize a human limb for a sufficient period and it will wither and mortify. An analogous situation will prevail if a human being is "immobilized," if there is no personal involvement in interests and activities, no participation in pursuits that are productive of some sort of visible results. The individual himself withers and mortifies; the fire in the furnace —untended because it serves no constructive purpose—flickers out.

Much, as I've said, is in the mind—or, more accurately, in the making up of one's mind whether one will feel dejected at 40, defeated at 50 and discarded at 60 or will continue to feel and think "young" at all ages.

The sooner the decision is made, the better—and the better the chances for success in all respects and regards.

6 ACCENTUATING THE PHYSICAL

The human body is a complex mechanism—and, as with all such mechanisms, the proverbial ounce of preventive maintenance is usually worth many pounds of "repair" or "cure." Each individual has a responsibility unto himself, a responsibility to ensure that he or she remains physically fit and healthy throughout life. Good health cannot be taken for granted. But we are very fortunate today, for we can do much to stay physically fit and we have an imposing array of aids and facilities available to us.

L et us return to the Holmesian simile of furnace and human body.

Most certainly, before any fires are kindled in the grate, it should be ascertained that the furnace itself is sturdily constructed, and it should be maintained in excellent working order. If it can be properly said that human beings owe duties and responsibilities to themselves, then the foremost of these unquestionably lie in safeguarding and maintaining their physical health and fitness. Whether one is naturally born with good health and a sturdy physique or acquires these assets later, the boons—like all things of great value—should be appreciated for their worth and preserved and protected with all possible care and effort.

Much of the course of one's life runs in channels dictated by the state of physical health. Generally speaking—though there have been many notable exceptions—an individual's achievements and accomplishments bear a distinct relationship to his or her physical condition and capacities, which may best be molded early in life.

"To be hale and hearty at eighty, one ought to start looking after his health long before he reaches the age of eight," I once heard a prominent physician declare.

The statement, I am sure, was rhetorical and exaggerated for the sake of emphasis. A child of such tender years possesses neither the foresight nor the capacity for independent decision necessary to begin taking the steps to ensure that he will remain healthy for seven or eight decades. On the other hand, it surely is within the power of his parents to help him establish the habits and patterns that will make him a fit and flourishing child and, later, adult.

But there is no quarreling with the fundamental principles implied by the doctor's remark. Any individual who hopes to enjoy robust health throughout his lifetime should "start looking after his health" at an early age and continue to do so as he grows older.

In this day and age, the task of achieving and maintaining optimum salubrity is much simpler than it was in and for past generations. As we have observed earlier, the advances of medical science and the immense improvements in general health standards endow our citizens with great starting-off-point advantages not enjoyed by their forebears. However, this does not confer an ironclad warrant of good health to every—or any—human being. Each person must still do his or her part, contributing no small or insignificant share toward developing a strong and fit constitution.

In short, *your* health and physical well-being are primarily your own responsibility and concern, partially under your control—yours to have, hold, improve, impair or destroy.

Yes, there are excellent doctors, specialists, clinics, hospitals, agencies and facilities at your disposal. They are qualified and equipped to examine, diagnose, treat and cure—but they can do little without the full cooperation of the individual. And, with all the medical knowledge and scientific marvels at your disposal, it is worse than merely lax and lackadaisical for you to fail to take full advantage of them for your own benefit.

At this point, I want to make it crystal clear that I am not a physician—and no one but a qualified medical authority can give *any* person medical advice or counsel. However, I believe that one may safely discuss the broad, common-sense rules which aid the average person in attaining and maintaining the peak of physical fitness, in keeping the "furnace" in good condition.

I myself have been a staunch advocate of "keeping fit" for as long as I can remember. Balanced diet, ample and vigorous exercise, plenty of fresh air—these are some of the rather prosaic components of my lifetime regimen for keeping my own furnace in the best possible operating condition. Boxing, wrestling, weight lifting, swimming, long walks and hikes, such games as football and tennis—all, I am firmly convinced, did their share in helping me to remain healthy.

The diary I kept as a child contains innumerable entries like the following selected at random from the year 1904, when I was eleven:

- May 25: "Boxing lessons at Minneapolis Club. Fine big room with punch [*sic*] bags."
- August 6: "Had a fine time of it boxing. Lessons increased."
- September 23: "Football."
- December 25: "Skating."

As the years passed, somehow I always managed to find—or make—time to indulge in some sort of active physical exercise. Even today, I still swim and take long walks.

I do not suggest that mine is or has been the sole or universally advantageous formula. Each individual—subject to his physician's instructions and recommendations—will evolve his own.

Oliver Wendell Holmes extolled the beneficial virtues of boating and rowing. The late Senator Theodore Green—who lived to be 98—played tennis and worked out in the Senate gymnasium until he was well into his eighties (but at 82, on doctor's orders, he finally forsook one of his favorite sports:

high diving). At the other extreme, General Douglas Mac-Arthur managed to remain a rock-hard physical specimen even though—according to John Gunther—he never indulged in any exercise. Gunther says the General attributed his excellent physical condition to three things: a regular daily afternoon nap, abstemiousness and the rare ability to fall asleep "almost instantly."

But whatever one finds is the most salutary regimen, he or she should follow it closely and carefully. There is neither reason nor excuse for letting things slide, for trying to maintain one's physical health in fits and starts. If something—be it daily deep-breathing or setting-up exercises, a reducing diet or whatever—needs to be done or is worth doing, it is folly to do it halfheartedly or sporadically.

Then, one is wont to comment on the ironic aspects of our affluent age with all its scientific and medical wonders.

First, there is the tendency on the part of many people to take good health for granted. Their attitude seems to be: "Why should I worry? If something goes wrong, my doctor can fix me up in a jiffy with a few pills or a couple of shots."

This outlook completely ignores the truism that—be it furnace or human body—preventive maintenance is far easier and more economical (to say nothing of it being far more efficient in the long run) than having repairs made after breakdowns occur.

Oddly enough, the same person who will pamper an automobile, taking it regularly to a service station or garage for periodic oil change, greasing and checkup, will very often shun going to the family doctor for the same analogous purposes.

The intelligent car owner who hears a knock in his engine is not going to wait until he burns out a main bearing before seeking the advice of a good mechanic. Yet innumerable supposedly intelligent persons will allow "knocks" in their bodies to get progressively worse and worse before they will consult a physician.

A second paradoxical deterrent to good health and physical fitness nowadays is the very fact that the physical labors and exertions once demanded of most people have greatly decreased, frequently to the vanishing point. Jobs have become more sedentary, and hence the individual obtains less exercise, has less opportunity to "work out" his muscles, allow his lungs to receive their full ration of oxygen and otherwise prevent his body from becoming stale and flabby.

Our affluent age is, I fear, also a rather effete age. Rarely does one walk to the nearest drugstore anymore. One simply takes ten steps to the garage, climbs into one's automobile and drives the few hundred yards to buy a tube of toothpaste or a bottle of nail polish.

For many men, about the only exercise they obtain is an occasional desultory game of golf—with most of the real exertion taking place in the elbow bending and jaw movement at the nineteenth hole. For many women, household chores entail little more effort than flicking the switches on various home appliances.

Is all this beneficial and conducive to physical fitness? Although I repeat that I am no medical authority, I rather doubt it. I have seen far too many hollow-chested, pasty-faced men with flabby muscles at 30, far too many women who are forced periodically to go on "crash" diets in a frantic effort to lose excess weight, to believe that the sedentary life is a salubrious one.

Then, there are indications that our affluent age is having even more pernicious and debilitating effects on some members of our population. Despite the presence of the factors which make this potentially the healthiest era in all history, professional observers deplore the skyrocketing rise in illnesses and diseases which stem primarily from emotional stresses—the so-called psychosomatic illnesses.

Such scientific investigations as the now classic intensive study made by Dr. Richard E. Gordon and Katherine K. Gordon (see their book *The Split-Level Trap*) have demonstrated that the good and easy life is not always a blessing for some people. They and other medical and psychiatric authorities report that, in many cases, as the standard of living goes up, so rises the incidence of such diseases and illnesses as ulcers, hypertension, coronary thrombosis and hypertensive cardiovascular disease. The experts lay the blame for these maladies squarely at the door of the emotional stresses produced by the mad scrambling and febrile status-seeking which characterize a not insignificant percentage of our flush, comfort-filled society.

Next come the out-and-out hypochondriacs—individuals whose illnesses, aches, pains and symptoms are entirely imaginary, who have absolutely no diagnosable physical problems. The most shocking aspect of hypochondria is that some leading authorities have estimated that *over 50 percent* of all Americans who consult doctors each year are in this category. They are hypochondriacs of various types and kinds—and physicians who tell them the truth gain nothing by their honesty.

"Hell hath no fury like a hypochondriac deprived of his pet symptoms," Dr. Karl Menninger of the famous Menninger Clinic has been quoted as commenting glumly.

Hypochondria, according to the medical consensus, is not limited to the status-seeker or rung-climber. It cuts across all financial, educational, occupational, environmental and age lines and levels.

There appears justification for the theory that emotionally caused illnesses and hypochondria have become two major classifications of "maladies" afflicting our populace.

Is it that Nature, abhorring as it does a vacuum, has caused emotionally based disease and hypochondria to rush in where real disease, plague and pestilence have been eradicated?

Or is it, perhaps, that people, still in a transitional stage and not yet fully acclimated to the comparatively much greater leisure and luxury of our era, are "spontaneously generating" their own substitutes for dangers and hardships?

The answers to these questions, if they are to be found, must come from physicians, psychiatrists, psychologists and sociologists. By no stretch of the imagination do they lie within the ken of the layman. Nonetheless, they offer fascinating—if not especially cheering or pleasant—food for thought and speculation.

Whatever the case, there is widespread agreement that a very close relationship exists between an individual's physical, mental and emotional health and well-being and his or her career and work situations. The latter not only affect the former for the employed person, but also have strong effects on the individual's family.

For this reason, you and your work is a subject that deserves closer examination. Therein lie many clues for achieving and maintaining your physical health.

7   A DOUBLE PORTION OF
DESSERT

"Today, all diseases are psychosomatic," Dr. William C. Menninger has been quoted as saying. "Any kind of symptom—a headache, a fear, hypochondria—is part of the total patient." Unfortunately, our present, fast-paced era poses its own special problems in the form of increased emotional stresses and anxieties which can cause or aggravate certain illnesses. But the intelligent individual combats the causes and minimizes the effects. After all, some of the individuals who have worked the hardest and made the greatest contributions to civilization lived decades beyond the average life span of their times. By following their example, you, too, can accomplish much and still live a long time—thereby adding a double portion of dessert to the meat and potatoes of your life.

Butcher, baker, candlestick maker . . .
   Rich man, poor man . . .
  Tom, Dick—and Harriet . . .
From the beginning of their working careers until retirement, the health of each and all is to some degree influenced by occupation or profession, work situations and environments. To start with, let us consider a handful of prima facie illustrations.

Some jobs are more liable to be detrimental to physical health or dangerous to life and limb than others (even life-insurance premiums may vary considerably according to one's occupation). And, notwithstanding safeguards, safety measures and sweeping preventive-medicine programs sponsored and provided by government and business and industry, there are still about 3,000 occupational diseases—maladies resulting directly from the work certain individuals perform. Luckily, the majority are nonfatal and rarely have permanently disabling effects; the United States Public Health Service estimates that more than three-quarters are dermatological in nature, caused by contact with skin-irritant substances.

Furthermore, despite the concerted and commendable efforts that have slashed the incidence of industrial accidents by more than 75 percent in the last 40 years, there are still some 2.4 million accidental injuries "at work" annually. Of these, about 19,000 prove fatal; some 60,000 result in permanent impairment to the victims.

(In fairness, it should be pointed out that motor-vehicle accidents cause more than twice as many deaths as industrial accidents, and that accidents in the home are nearly double the number at work and result in over 50 percent more fatalities each year.)

Purely occupational illnesses and accidents are, of course, immediately identifiable and may be statistically tabulated as such. There is no question about a case of dermatitis that develops from contact with a caustic solution in a processing plant or a broken ankle suffered by a workman who falls off a ladder while doing his job in a factory. These are clearly work-connected.

However, there are less sharply defined and less readily recognizable areas of occupational health hazards and illnesses.

For example, unbeknownst to himself or anyone else, an individual may not be physically suited for the work he performs. He may have some defect or suffer from some condition that makes it inadvisable—or downright dangerous—for him to perform the tasks demanded of him. It is to prevent such mésalliances between work and worker that many companies require prospective employees to undergo medical examinations and meet specified physical criteria for certain types of work.

In some fields, rigorous periodic physical examinations are mandatory; those taken by airline flight personnel spring to mind immediately as illustrations. Nowadays, even many corporations demand that their executives take regular medical examinations, often at company expense. In short, business and industry are acutely aware that a healthy employee—be he top-level manager or bottom-rung maintenance man—is an asset, while an unhealthy employee can be a costly liability. Each year, United States industry loses somewhere in the neighborhood of 600 million man (and woman) days due to illness; the financial loss this represents can be calculated in the billions of dollars.

But our present interest is in the manner in which an individual's occupation and work situation may affect his physical, mental and emotional health.

One does not need a medical degree to appreciate that unusual or excessive mental and emotional stresses and strains a person may encounter in his work will drain his stamina, lower his resistance and create fertile psychological ground in which real or imagined maladies quickly take root and flourish. The man or woman who is chronically unhappy—or "miserable"—in his or her occupation or work situation is not likely to be bursting with radiant all-around good health very long.

"Today, all diseases are psychosomatic," Dr. William C. Menninger stated a few years ago. "Any kind of symptom—a headache, a fear, hypochondria—is part of the total patient. Psychosomatic still means both mind and body, but in a wider sense it includes all the inner and outer forces that animate his personality. We have to treat the man, not the pieces or parts."

Most authorities agree that the average person's occupation and work situation are among the important "outer forces that animate his personality." If these are not salutary they may well generate pernicious "inner forces" within the individual, producing what physicians and psychiatrists call "anxiety states."

What are "anxiety states" or "anxieties"?

Here is an explanation supplied by Dr. Harry R. Lipton in the *Handbook of Correctional Psychology:*

"The root element of anxiety is the emotion of fear . . . fear of failure and of inadequacy, fear of not being equal to the demands that will be made upon one."

A 1960 report—issued by a leading United States ethical-drug concern and based on data obtained from medical journals—estimated that 13 percent of all "workers" and 19 percent of all "executives" suffered from "anxiety states." These figures will hardly come as a surprise to anyone who has observed how, in their work, so very many people are obviously beset by the kinds of fears Dr. Lipton describes.

Although essentially *psycho*logical, anxieties are not without their *physio*logical effects and repercussions.

"Anxiety is commonly accompanied by physical symptoms," Dr. Lipton writes. "Headache, nervousness, insomnia, heartburn and shortness of breath are common. A heavy feeling in the chest, a feeling of pressure or of pain may be experienced. Palpitation may . . . be present. . . ."

Nor does that constitute the sum. Prolonged worries and emotional stresses—"anxieties"—are said to be among the causative or aggravating factors in such ailments as peptic ulcers, essential hypertension and even arteriosclerosis.

In other words, it is not stretching the point much to say that an individual whose occupation or work situation is a source of constant fear, frustration or irritation is not only harming his health, but is also gravely reducing his chances of living a long—to say nothing of a happy—life.

Yet some individuals persist in disregarding all psychological and physiological warning signals. They will remain in bad work situations and will drive themselves beyond the limits of common sense and endurance, frequently driving themselves right out of productive existence and into a hospital bed or worse.

Naturally, almost everyone wants to "make good," to succeed, gain more pay, perquisites and prestige. But to make a shambles of one's health in the process is not only madness, it is totally unnecessary.

"You can't knock 'em dead if you kill yourself trying," is the breezy—but trenchant—motto a highly successful sales manager displays prominently in the room where he holds meetings with his salesmen.

The admonition applies in all fields of endeavor. Accomplishment and achievement seldom equate with emotional rack and physical ruin. Effort, attainment and success are fully compatible with excellent health and longevity.

In these pages, we have already made brief, passing acquaintance with the names of several men and women who accomplished much and lived long. It will not hurt to mention a random few more and thereby drive the point further home.

Consider the ripe ages reached by these famous Americans who made great contributions in various fields:

- **Educators:** Roscoe Pound, 94; John Dewey, 93; Mark Hopkins, 85.
- **Inventors:** Thomas A. Edison, 84; Samuel F. B. Morse, 81; Lee De Forest, 87.
- **Industrialists and businessmen:** John D. Rockefeller, 98; George L. Hartford and Samuel H. Kress, both 92.

Such men as these encountered countless and great problems and setbacks in their careers. Nevertheless, they overcame all obstacles and were successful without driving themselves into early graves. There is no real reason why the average person cannot do the same, why he cannot reach his goals—and go beyond them—without adversely affecting his physical health and well-being.

It is understood that most people must work. What is not so well understood is that they must work not only to earn their livelihood, but also because work satisfies a basic psychological need for productive activity. Since the average person must—and will—work for many years, he should do all in his power to do the type of work that will enhance rather than detract from his life and the gratification he derives from living.

As I noted earlier, a person might not always be able to follow precisely the career he most desires; but, if the ideal is out of reach, a satisfactory alternative or reasonable compromise is usually feasible. At very least, within whatever limits are imposed upon him, an individual should always seek to select the type of work that comes closest to suiting his tastes and desires and which he has the greatest chance of enjoying.

Only thus can anyone hope to reduce any potential frustration factor and minimize the possibility of finding himself getting deeper and deeper into an anxiety-ridden, emotion-straining and health-destroying career furrow.

There will be problems and difficulties, temporary periods of discouragement and dismay in any field of endeavor or on any job. These must be accepted as part of the "day's" work. It is ridiculous to advise anyone "not to worry," for everyone will sometimes have to "worry" about his work, pondering what he is doing and whether he is doing it correctly, planning the next steps and thinking to the future.

On the other hand, if a particular work situation or environment proves hopelessly unsatisfactory, causes heavy and protracted mental and emotional strain and an inordinate drain on his physical health, the intelligent individual will not hesitate to make a change. He will not be a "rat" for deserting the sinking ship, but a wise and prudent person rightly obeying his instincts for self-preservation.

True, it might be difficult to make a change. It might well cost effort, time and money, but these expenditures are bargain bagatelles compared to the cost of obdurately "sticking" and paying an exorbitant price in emotional and physical illness or breakdown.

This is not to argue against anyone's working hard. Far from it. An individual should work to the reasonable maximum of his capacity. But there is a whole universe of difference between working hard and making progress, and exertion that merely batters a person's energy and vitality out against the stone wall of what for him, at any rate, is an intolerable or untenable work situation.

Then, regardless of how ambitious and energetic an individual may be, he must always remember that he is not a perpetual-motion machine. He cannot work constantly, without rest and relaxation, and expect to stay effective and healthy. Really successful people, the ones who accomplish the most, realize the need for an occasional break in pace, a pause to restore and refresh themselves.

A constructive attitude toward one's work or job is another

very important factor in maintaining health, strength and vigor. Agreed that no one can be constantly cheerful and optimistic, bubbling over with goodwill and beaming with smiles. At the same time, only an exceedingly stupid (and largely useless) person will always groan and moan, carp and complain; that is the most direct route to sour, dour and premature dotage.

The frame of mind an individual adopts toward his work is extremely important from the very beginning of his career. It becomes even more important as the years pass—and begins to reach its peak as the time for retirement draws near.

What attitude has the individual formed toward retirement?

Has he made the hideous and senseless mistake of viewing it as the finish of his active, productive life, thereby guaranteeing rapid deterioration of health and loss of vigor and vitality?

Or does he see that retirement is not the end of anything but one single stage or period—and the beginning of another, during which he can freely build, create and enjoy?

The man who has formed *this* attitude has not lost his health or grown old or stale on the job. He has remained young and vital, and he will savor the fresh adventure of a new and rewarding life. The infinite variety of pursuits and pleasures that await him are succinctly described by Clarence B. Randall in his fine book, *The Folklore of Management*.

"The man who cheerfully accepts retirement and enters with genuine enthusiasm into the reorientation of his life . . . can select from his deferred agenda the activity which excites him most," Randall writes, "and he can also establish his own tempo and rhythm in doing it. He can work part-time or full-time as he pleases, and can alternate almost at will his periods of activity with those of rest and relaxation."

People with such attitudes are like physicians who, rather than "healing themselves," have been practicing their own preventive medicine throughout their careers. They have doubtless done excellent jobs but, in addition, they have used their work as an invigorator and rejuvenator to keep them fresh, hale and hearty—and they will remain so for a long time to come.

To them, the years that have passed were the meat and potatoes.

Having retained their healthy appetite—and capacity—for life and living, for them retirement and what lies beyond constitute a mouth-watering double portion of dessert.

8 EXTRACURRICULAR INTERESTS AS INVIGORATORS

All work and no play makes Jack (or Jill) dull—but, conversely, all play and no work is liable to have an equally harmful effect. The answer is to strike a balance—to achieve a satisfying blend or "mix" of work and nonvocational interests. As an example, my own recipe—how I arrived at it and how I believe that it has had a beneficial influence on my own life. A few views and opinions on what the average person's outside interests can do to make for a fuller, more zestful life.

Human nature is filled with contradictions.

On the one hand, there is *homo faber*—man the maker —with a strong drive to work and create. Were it otherwise, we would not have progressed beyond the original primitive.

On the other, the average human being wants—indeed, requires—leisure, "extracurricular" interests and activities, diversions and amusements. These not only relieve his labors, rest and refresh his body but serve as rejuvenators and elasticizers of his mind and spirit.

I concur unreservedly with the proposition expressed in the familiar old saw about all work and no play making dull boys. At the same time, I can personally attest that the exact opposite is true, that all play sans the gratification obtained from constructive endeavor can—and will—make one as dull as, if not duller than, the converse.

I was not quite 24 when, after having a rare streak of good fortune in the Oklahoma oil fields, I suddenly discovered myself to be a rather wealthy young man. It seemed I had enough money to last me for life and, consequently, there appeared to be no need for doing any more work. I therefore decided to "retire," intending to spend my ensuing days and years in the carefree pursuit of pleasure.

This—with appropriate self-critical sarcasm I might call it my Hedonistic Period—proved to be brief and not at all what I had expected it would be. The delights of purely pleasure-orientated existence soon began to pall and then became a deadly bore. Whereupon, after little more than a year of indolence, I came out of my premature retirement and went back to work.

However, the interlude had not been entirely wasted; it served to teach me a valuable lesson and bring into proper focus many truths to which I had been previously exposed, but apparently had not taken to heart.

But perhaps it would be best if I interrupted my narrative and, before going further with it, doubled back to show just how my personal views and attitudes evolved.

First, there were the fundamentals my father sought to impress upon me, but which, in the manner of most men's sons, I did not immediately grasp and apply.

In regard to work, my father's basic operative credo was Sir Francis Bacon's *verbum sapienti:* "No man's fortune can be an end worthy of his being." It was on this foundation that he built his own philosophy.

I recall his once reading me the following passage from Plutarch's story of the life of Pompey:

When Pompey first landed his fleet near Carthage, 7,000 of the foe deserted to his army, which consisted of six legions at full strength. Then, they say, a somewhat absurd incident happened. Apparently, some of his soldiers came across a quantity of cached treasure and thus obtained a considerable sum of money. The story got abroad and the entire army fancied the region must be full of buried wealth which the Carthaginians had hidden. Pompey could do nothing with his soldiers for several days. He simply went about laughing as he saw so many thousands of troops digging up the ground and turning it over, until in the end they got tired of it and asked him to lead them wherever he wished. They told him they had suffered enough for their folly.

The moral, my father contended, was twofold. A person may, by stroke of luck, obtain wealth. But blind, frantic seeking after wealth for its own sake, as an end unto itself, often requires immense expenditures of effort without much return.

"The important thing is not how much money you have, but what you do with it," he maintained. "If you are a businessman, both you and your money must continue to work— you as an active administrator of your wealth as working capital. Your job is to produce more goods and services for more people, create jobs for others and contribute to the general betterment of society. It's the only way a businessman can justify his wealth or his existence."

The truths finally penetrated after my short fling at "retirement," when I learned that if a person does no work at all and devotes himself to play, he experiences a painful feeling that something very important is missing from his life. Possibly it is merely as Josh Billings (Henry Wheeler Shaw) observed, that "few men have enough character to lead a life of idleness." It is, I suppose, equally possible that the psychiatrists are correct when they argue that people who do nothing but play suffer from a condition known as "pathological boredom with work."

Says Dr. Irving Bieber in the *American Journal of Psychotherapy*: "Such individuals are compelled by their anxieties to loaf about and 'putter' . . . finding ways of dissipating time. The occupation of a 'playboy' is not one of choice, inasmuch as the anxieties involved in work inhibitions are manifestations of a profound personality disturbance."

Whatever the answer, a total lack of work brought me nothing but boredom, restlessness and a sense of futility. And, it has been my observation, idleness has the same effect on most people.

But I am no less aware that—to borrow and mangle a phrase—man cannot live by work alone. People must have interests and pursuits outside their regular work if they are not to become stale and exhausted, dreary one-dimensional creatures who mentally as well as physically grow old long before their time.

In order to have any hope of fulfilling himself and enjoying life and living, each individual must strike a balance between work and play. In my own case, the lessons I learned and my experience and experiences led me to formulate a personal line of reasoning which is roughly as follows:

1. I, being a businessman, must work and must make the greatest share of my money work as capital to build and expand my business enterprises.

2. However, if I concentrate solely on work, I not only narrow my perspectives and reduce my effectiveness, but I will derive very little enjoyment from living.

3. Ergo, the only sensible solution is to follow a course which permits me to simultaneously work *and* live to the utmost, to enjoy a rounded existence.

The average person should not encounter much difficulty "finding" the outside interests to round his existence. Naturally, any working person's "extracurricular" pursuits are primarily intended to provide immediate enjoyment and gratification. Nonetheless—and we might as well all admit it—in the back of practically every mind there lurks the anticipatory thought that these will prove of particular value in later years, when the individual is ready and qualified for mature retirement.

It doesn't matter what forms one's interests and activities take. They can run the alphabetical gamut from aardvark-breeding to the study of Zoroastrianism. They can go from the ridiculous of collecting empty milk cartons to the sublime of amateur astronomy, from the completely nonfunctional to the ultrautilitarian. What counts are the individual's degree of commitment and personal involvement and the amount of pleasure and satisfaction leisure-time pursuits provide.

The number and variety of an individual's activities are governed only by himself and his capacities. And, seeming paradox that it is, very often the people with the heaviest work loads and greatest responsibilities have the largest number and the most diversified extracurricular interests. William Hazlitt noted this more than 150 years ago, when he wrote:

"The more we do, the more we can; the more busy we are, the more leisure we have."

This is easily understood. Able, productive individuals know how to organize their work—and themselves. They know how to set a pace and tempo that will allow them to accomplish all their allotted tasks without extraneous fuss, commotion or any waste of time. They thereby have more time and energy, vim and enthusiasm left over for doing other things they like or find challenging or rewarding.

A person will probably develop several interests early in life —as early as his childhood. Some of these he may retain throughout the years; others may be modified or refined, expanded in scope or shifted to related fields. Yet others may be discarded altogether.

Once more to use myself as an example, when a boy I had many interests in addition to the sports and athletics I've already mentioned. Among other things, I collected postage stamps, read avidly and was fascinated by all that had to do with that then still fairly newfangled gadget the automobile. I eagerly collected and traded the catalogues, maintenance manuals and similar literature issued by motorcar manufacturers.

Of these particular boyhood leisure activities, only one has survived over the intervening years. For some unaccountable reason, my stamp-collecting hobby withered, and I never became a full-blown philatelist. And, as automobiles lost their novelty and I gained a fair working knowledge of the mechanical principles and general characteristics common to all makes, the catalogues and maintenance manuals gradually lost their appeal. But I did retain a voracious appetite for reading (including, it must be confessed, a taste for occasional and nostalgic rereading of my boyhood favorites, the prolific G. A. Henty's adventure novels, of which I have a treasured collection).

As time passed, I—like most people—developed a miscellany of interests, some more or less transient or frivolous, others that proved serious and permanent. For instance, I have taken lessons to keep up with the latest dance steps and lessons to learn celestial navigation. I've undertaken to study music and to trace down all the information available about events or personalities that fascinated me in various periods of history. I've tried my hand at photography (I will never be another Steichen or Bachrach) and conducted culinary experiments in my kitchen (my pancakes and waffles are edible, but it's doubtful if much more can be said for them). Although my ambition to enter the Diplomatic Corps had to be abandoned, I have been lucky enough to travel and see a good bit of the world, have learned a few foreign languages —and managed to satisfy at least partially my desire to write.

These are only a sampling of the interests and pursuits that have caught my fancy and to which I have turned my leisure-time energies over the years. But the clearest demonstration I can personally offer of how an extracurricular interest awakens, takes hold and expands into a highly gratifying avocational pursuit lies in the story of my activities and experiences as a collector of fine art. I propose—I hope with my readers' indulgence—to narrate the story in some detail.

No, I have no intentions of proselytizing, of trying to convince anyone that art collecting is *the* leisure-time pursuit for one and all, because I know very well it is not. The reasons for embarking on a detailed discourse about my collecting are much different.

First, the development of my interest in fine art is traceable step by step—and thus serves as a good representative case history of the manner in which *any* leisure-time pursuit can germinate and grow to fruition.

Second, my experiences may show others—by parallel and analogy—how much real, lasting satisfaction is to be derived from a nonwork-connected activity once the individual commits himself and there is deep personal involvement.

Third, the story proves that an individual's "hobby" can be beneficial not only to himself, but to others as well—and that this is a bonus of enjoyment and gratification.

Fourth, the narrative will, I think, prove how a genuine interest in any field expands all of one's horizons, adds depth and dimension to one's whole being and acts as a lifelong tonic and invigorator.

9 HOW A "HOBBY" IS BORN— AND CAN CHANGE ONE'S ENTIRE LIFE

Using my own experience as an example, I explore the birth and growth of an extracurricular interest. The story of how a trip to the Orient in 1912—and the expenditure of a few dollars—eventually led me to become a serious collector of fine art. The urge and desire needed many years to develop, but the end results have been worth all the time, effort and money I have expended. Some of the invaluable lessons my slow-blooming interest in art collecting has taught me about an individual's instinctive need to become personally involved in activities apart and aside from his everyday work.

In 1912, I visited the Orient, touring Japan and China. During my trip, I bought some oddments of carved ivory and examples of Chinese bronze-work and lacquer; my total expenditure for all was considerably less than one hundred dollars.

Albeit I purchased the items more as souvenirs of my voyage than as art, it could be said that these acquisitions represented my first forays into the field of art collecting. And they were also my last, for fully eighteen years. It wasn't until 1930 that I picked up the slender threads I had dropped in the Orient almost two decades before.

As has been the case with many other people, my interest in fine art did not really start to awaken until I had matured. It was not until then that a deep appreciation for and a strong desire to collect art began to manifest themselves.

At that, the "second beginnings" were modest enough. In 1930, I purchased a painting by the seventeenth-century Dutch artist Jan van Goyen. However, once kindled, my interest and enthusiasm swiftly flared up; within a very few more years, I was committed—an active and serious collector.

It must be confessed that the conditions prevailing during the early and mid-1930s were conducive to increasing any collector's zeal. The 1929 stock market "crash" and the depression that followed caused many hands that formerly held a firm grip on choice works of art to relax their hold. Where, formerly, museum-quality examples of fine art had all but vanished from the market—having been purchased at enormous prices by extremely wealthy individuals or heavily endowed public institutions—they now began to turn up for sale. And the prices asked or realized for them were often only a minute fraction of what their owners had paid and far below even the most conservatively estimated actual values of the items.

For example, at the 1933 Thomas Fortune Ryan sale at the Anderson Gallery in New York City, I purchased ten paintings by the Spanish Impressionist Joaquín Sorolla y Bastida. Less than five years later, conservative expert appraisal placed their market value at more than four times what I'd paid for them!

In the late 1930's, although the United States had begun to see many signs of economic recovery, new and ominous factors opened up great additional reservoirs of art that had been previously considered impregnable. These were some of the great private European collections, and it was the gathering threat of war that caused their owners to sell and realize cash for their precious belongings.

The menace of war caused apprehension and fear that frequently verged on panic, and, again, superb items were sold for comparatively small—quite often virtually negligible—sums. Thus, in 1938, at a sale in the Netherlands, I was able to purchase Rembrandt's magnificent "Portrait of Marten Looten" for less than one-half the price its prior owner paid for it a decade earlier. That same year, at another sale, in London, I acquired a large (114 by 64 inch) portrait of Louis XIV by Hyacinthe Rigaud for about $700. It was, incidentally, at the same sale that I bought—for $200—a panel that later proved to be Raphael's long-lost masterpiece the "Madonna of Loreto," worth an astronomical price.

The outbreak of World War II brought my collecting to an almost complete halt for several years. My attention was concentrated first on the vital wartime output of my business interests and later, after V-J Day, on their reconversion to peacetime production. But, having been infected by the virus, I proved to have a chronic disease and not even the long interruption helped cure it. As soon as conditions permitted, I resumed my collecting, even though the art market throughout the world had not only firmed but started a new upward spiral. That steady climb, it might be noted *en passant,* has continued to the present day and gives no indication of stopping in the foreseeable future.

Now, I think I should make clear at the start that, in the early 1930s, I—like so many other tyro collectors—was not entirely certain in which directions my tastes and bents lay. Nonetheless, although there have been detours and digressions, the patterns were not long in forming. As I gained knowledge and experience, my collector's interest and enthusiasm channeled themselves chiefly into five major categories:

1. Ancient Greek and Roman marbles and bronzes.
2. Renaissance paintings.
3. Sixteenth-century Persian carpets.
4. Savonnerie carpets.
5. Eighteenth-century French furniture and tapestries (with some rather noteworthy excursions into the fields of eighteenth-century English portraiture and French paintings of the same period).

I've found—through personal experience and observation —that interests in which an individual deeply involves himself are governed by a sort of Parkinsonian Law in that they have the effect of developing and multiplying related interests by the square. So it most certainly is with art collecting; some hint of how the collector feels is contained in a paragraph written by Ethel Le Vane in the book *Collector's Choice*, a few years ago:

"To me, my works of art are all vividly alive. They are the embodiment of whoever created them—a mirror of their creator's hopes and dreams, aspirations and frustrations."

Each chronological period, the artists, their contemporaries and subjects come to life, and the collector is motivated to learn all he can about each and all. Stated another way, the collector is not satisfied or content until he can project himself into history, becoming almost as familiar with the people, life, customs, problems and characteristics of past periods as he is with those of his own time and place.

Obviously, space will not permit extensive discussion of all five categories of my collection. I shall select only one, the last, because it deals with that splendid historical era to which I've made so many references, the eighteenth century. Perhaps I will be able thereby to impart some idea of how a collector's imagination is captured by a given historical period and how, by knowing its arts, he reaps the rich rewards of erasing time barriers and feeling as though he is actually able to project himself into the period and be part of it. . . .

The eighteenth century was the age of the Rococo, of boudoirs, of *fêtes galantes*—and its painters often appear to have greater attraction than some of the more profound painters of earlier and later periods. Some evidence of this is furnished by the fantastic prices paid by this generation for the works of Gainsborough, Romney, Watteau, Boucher, Fragonard and other eighteenth-century masters. Lord Duveen once said to me, in 1938, that if the portrait by Gainsborough of Perdita Robinson, owned by the Wallace Collection in London, were auctioned, he would open the bidding with an offer of £200,000—a million dollars then. Gainsborough's "Blue Boy" was sold in 1928 for $750,000, and Lord Duveen told me that shortly afterward he offered to buy back the picture for $825,000 but his offer was refused. It might be mentioned here that this picture was purchased by John Hoppner for

65 guineas (then roughly $350) in 1803, after having been sold for 36 guineas in 1796.

Painting in the seventeenth century is represented by the profound works of Rembrandt and Velásquez, in the nineteenth century by the scientific masterpieces of the French Impressionists. In the eighteenth century painting was represented by the delicacy and charm of Watteau, Boucher and Fragonard in France; and Gainsborough, Romney and Reynolds in England. The seventeenth century was the age of the soldier and the cleric, the nineteenth of the bourgeois and the eighteenth of the gay courtier.

France set the fashion in art during the entire eighteenth century. No other country could match her in good architects, painters, sculptors, designers and decorators, nor in skilled artisans. They were all dominated in the first half of the century by the florid and fantastic spirit of the Rococo, which was a revolt against the pompous decayed classicism of the Louis XIV period. Watteau became the founder, and at the same time the culmination, of the new French school. He is considered today by many authorities to be the greatest painter of the eighteenth century; but his genius was unrecognized for many generations. During the last years of his life Watteau's art was highly esteemed; but from the middle of the eighteenth century to about 1875, his pictures were held in such slight esteem that the prices realized by them at public auction rarely exceeded $500. The finest collection of Watteau's works belonged to the deposed German Kaiser. The Wallace Collection and the Louvre each have nine of his paintings.

The best-known artist of the eighteenth century was Boucher. His art was an apotheosis of the Rococo. His usual subjects are scenes from the story of Cupid and Psyche, Galatea encircled by Cupids or the deserted Ariadne. Everything is light and rosy, corresponding to the interior decorations of the Louis XV period. Boucher led the life of a grand seigneur, spent tremendous sums, subsidized ballet dancers and gave artistic fêtes to which the fashionable world of Paris flocked. He possessed an artistic collection including goldsmiths' work, bronzes, Japanese wood engravings, Chinese porcelains, besides pictures and drawings by many great masters. The period of his activity covers half a century. Up to the last day of his life (he lived to be 68), he worked ten hours a day, and under the government of Pompadour especially he was the man for everything. Every day, he appeared at the palace to give her instructions in painting. No court festival, no theatrical representation took place which he did not conduct. He designed the costumes for the great ladies who appeared at the court. Inexhaustible in invention, he furnished designs for sculptors, ivory carvers, goldsmiths and carpenters; for wallpaper, furniture, sedan chairs, bookbindings, fans and jewelry. He molded porcelain figures and mantel decorations, vases and chandeliers.

He painted easel pictures and wall or ceiling pictures, screens and carriage doors. He was the greatest interior decorator of his day, and hundreds of rooms in Paris, Versailles and elsewhere were decorated by him. He typifies better than anyone else the luxurious life of the Rococo.

Fragonard, like Watteau, was popular during his lifetime but forgotten after his death. In the last years of the nineteenth century he regained the position among the masters of painting to which he is entitled by his genius. His most famous painting is "The Swing," in the Wallace Collection.

France produced many other able painters during the eighteenth century, including: Chardin, Latour, Pater, Lancret, Rigaud, Greuze, Vigée-Lebrun, Le Prince and Nattier. The variety and genius of French painters gave France the leading place in painting early in the eighteenth century, and this preeminence France has maintained ever since.

Painting in England during the eighteenth century was remarkable chiefly for portraiture. The English, like the Dutch, were willing to give commissions to portrait painters. In the seventeenth century the demand had been met by foreigners, of whom the most eminent were Vandyck and Lely.

By the middle of the eighteenth century, English portrait painters were ready to garner the harvest. Gainsborough, Reynolds and Romney are three of the foremost portrait painters of all time. Their portraits have much in common for one judging them in this age. Their subjects have the calmness and sureness, the leisurely grace and courtly manners of a bygone age. Their daily costumes make our modern dress seem very plain and bourgeois. It was an era of great portrait painters and it must be admitted that the costumes of the time were favorable to artistic portraits.

Gainsborough, Reynolds and Romney painted altogether some 2,000 portraits, and they had a reputation among their contemporaries of always securing a good likeness.

I have been fortunate in securing examples of the work of each of these artists for my collection. Gainsborough is represented by the "Portrait of James A. Christie"—called "one of the really great English portraits" by art authority Dr. Julius Held—and the "Portrait of the Countess of Chesterfield." Reynolds is represented by his "Portrait of Joanna Leigh," and Romney by his "Dutchess of Cumberland."

It has sometimes been asserted that the art of portrait painting does not consist in securing a likeness, but in producing a work of art. I hold this view to be incorrect. A portrait is a likeness; whether it is called a work of art has nothing to do with the matter. If a painter secures a likeness, he is entitled to call it a portrait. If he does not secure a likeness, it may be a work of art, but it is not a portrait. Moreover, the importance of a likeness is often much greater than that of a work of art, especially in the case of famous men and women of history. We are accustomed to judging people's character, motives and ability by looking at them. A good likeness of Julius Caesar or of Cleopatra would be of more interest to us than many pages of their history. It is difficult to understand a person one has never seen. When we do see a person in whom we are interested we want to see him or her in good light, and exactly as he or she is. We want to know how Julius Caesar and Cleopatra really looked, not how some artist *thought* they should look. Anyone who has ever had experience with portrait painters will readily admit that it is much easier to secure a so-called interesting or artistic portrait than it is to secure a good likeness. The eye is very cunning when it is trained and we are all trained to observe faces. The slightest variance from reality is instantly noted. There can be no higher, nor more difficult, goal in portrait painting than to secure a good likeness. Let those who refuse to subscribe to this cease to call themselves portrait painters.

Gainsborough, Reynolds and Romney had formidable rivals in Raeburn, Hoppner and Lawrence. In fact, in the last twenty years of the century they were less popular than the younger artists. Besides the portraitists, England had an excellent painter in Hogarth, who painted scenes of the daily life of the common people. His work is distinguished by cynical humor, biting—and sometimes vicious—satire and the pointing of a moral.

Germany, the mighty music master of the eighteenth century, was but a feeble child in painting. The Flemish and Dutch masters of the seventeenth century left no heirs and painting in the Low Countries during the eighteenth century was at a low ebb. The glorious sun of the seventeenth and earlier centuries had apparently set forever.

Italy, however, produced one great painter. Venetian art, once so glorified by Titian, Giorgione and Veronese, had seemed extinct for over a century when Tiepolo, as though by a miracle, revived it. Although he ranks with Veronese in artistic ability, he is a true child of the eighteenth century— free, nonchalant, bold, sparkling. The more solid qualities of Veronese—depth of thought and balance of design—are often wanting in Tiepolo's work, but he surpasses Veronese in perspective and equals him in color. Many churches and *palazzi* in Venice have walls and ceilings painted by him. Some of his finest work is in the Archbishop's palace at Würzburg. Apart from Tiepolo, Italy had many competent painters and it must not be forgotten that Boucher, Fragonard, Greuze and Vigée-Lebrun studied for years in Rome.

Spain, too, produced a solitary painter of first rank in the eighteenth century. Goya, a worthy successor of Velásquez, did not equal the older painter in calm mastery of the subject, but surpassed him in power and versatility. His most famous paintings are "La Maja Desnuda" and "La Maja Vestida," in Madrid.

But paintings form only a very small part of my "fifth-category" collection of eighteenth-century art. The bulk consists of very different items of two distinct types—one of which I, like countless others, never even dreamed to consider an art form before I began collecting.

Nevertheless, these things serve even better than paintings to bring a bygone era to life—and to illustrate how one interest will stimulate others, invigorating the individual and his intellect and adding breadth and depth to his whole existence.

10 A LESSON IN MULTIPLICATION —OF EXTRACURRICULAR INTERESTS

Continuing to use my own experience and experiences as examples, I try to show how, when a person becomes deeply involved in a given interest, he soon finds that it greatly broadens his horizons and leads him into new and exciting fields. We take a voyage in time —back to the eighteenth century—and, I hope, see how interests multiply and make one's existence more gratifying even while they increase one's knowledge and understanding of man and civilization.

Oddly enough, for the first forty or so years of my life, I paid little if any attention to furniture. To me, it was a largely utilitarian adjunct and, although I preferred it to be comfortable and pleasing to the eye, I hardly thought of it as an art form.

Then, in 1936, I went to New York City on a protracted visit in connection with my business affairs. It was necessary for me to rent suitable living accommodations, and I subleased an apartment from Mrs. Frederick Guest. This marked a turning point—or, perhaps, "awakening" would be a better and more accurate way of putting it.

Mrs. Guest, a lady of great personal charm, culture and taste, had furnished the apartment with a superb collection of eighteenth-century French and English furniture. Living, as I did for several months, in the exquisitely decorated and furnished surroundings, I could not help but begin to appreciate that a table, a chair, a cabinet or a commode could be as much a piece of fine art as a painting or a sculpture.

With the dawn of awareness and appreciation came the desire to know and understand more. I therefore began a cram course of heavy reading, supplementing it with long hours of conversation and discussion with authorities in the field and visits to museums and galleries where fine examples of the master furniture makers' art were on display. All this led—and with rather astonishing speed—to my developing a new, deep and lasting extracurricular interest, namely in eighteenth-century French furniture.

Why did I narrow down to the particular period and type?

The answer to that question once again demonstrates how an indvidual's "outside" interests develop, grow and expand, stretching his horizons and breeding additional interests.

My studies and researches proved that it can be safely said the eighteenth century was the golden age of furniture and that France reigned supreme. The Regency period (1715–23) introduced the Rococo style, and the interior decoration and furniture were made to match. Everyone was tired of the spacious stateliness of the palaces and homes of the previous reign. For the first time since antiquity, the interiors of houses were designed for comfort and charm rather than for pomp and show.

Everyone wanted comfort and small, intimate apartments and boudoirs became the rule. Dining rooms were introduced into house design. Formerly meals had been served in various rooms and a special dining room was hardly known. The furniture of the Regency period reflected the new style; straight lines were replaced by curves; everything was less massive; less monumental. The commode is an invention of the early eighteenth century and soon became very popular for it contributed to the comfort and elegance of the new interiors.

Under Louis XV, who reigned from 1723 to 1774, furniture became still more graceful, reflecting the feminine influence of Pompadour and Du Barry. Small *secrétaires* with fall fronts, small boudoir tables and *guéridons* became popular. Rolltop desks are an invention of this period, the classic example being the "Bureau de Roi" by Oeben and Riesener in the Louvre. It has been said that this is the most valuable piece of French furniture to come down to us and that it would probably fetch $500,000 or more at auction today. Louis XVI furniture is still delicate and feminine, but the taste of the time was classical and the curves of the Rococo were replaced by straight lines.

We cannot understand fine eighteenth-century French furniture unless we know how it was produced and are familiar with the aristocratic life of the time. Furniture was made by hand, and its production was a monopoly of the masters of the cabinetmakers' guild. These men served five or six years as apprentices and several more years as journeymen before they were ready to take their entrance examinations to the guild. The candidate for membership had to produce, unaided, a piece of furniture which in design, workmanship and quality was worthy of the traditions of the guild. A jury of masters delivered the verdict and if it was favorable, the candidate was elected to the guild and given the title of Master Cabinetmaker. The guild members, being monopolists, sought to restrict the membership by various means. One regulation was that no master should have more than two apprentices at a time.

Let us enter the shop of one of the Paris masters. It is small, about 20 by 40 feet, and only five men are working: the master, two journeymen and two apprentices. They are making a *bureau plat,* or library table, and the five men have been busy for a month on this table. Furthermore much of the work has been done by outside specialists.

The master of the shop is Benneman, and the year is 1785. The wood for the table was procured from the stocks of the guild and had been kept for twenty years in a dry place. The moisture was consequently out of it, and the wood was worthy of Master Benneman's skill. There is no machinery in the shop, yet no one feels the lack of it. On the contrary, there

is a deftness and artistry in the men's work that the mechanical
and arbitrary machine could never hope to equal. At last,
Benneman's table is finished, and he prepares to send it to
the wealthy man who ordered it, together with the following
bill:

A flat-topped table, 5'8" long, 2'4" wide, 2'6" high, richly
decorated in bronze and with rich *sabots* [table feet]:

Small-scale model in wax	96 *livres*
Full-size model of wax and wood for casting	300
Casting	498
Soldering	17
Sketch painting for the marqueterie workers showing fruits, flowers, etc.	168
Eight panels in marqueterie designed after sketch	442
Design	36
To Bardin for bronze chasing	1,200
Mounting	100
Morocco leather for table top	28
Gilding bronze, Galle	1,200
Gilding for morocco leather	13
Ebony and amaranth wood	150
Fifteen sheets of gray wood	15
Locksmith work	150
Day work of cabinetmakers	786
Day work of Benneman	508
Packing	9
TOTAL	5,716 *livres*

Since the livre was equivalent to the franc, Benneman's
bill was over $1,100—and money was then worth many times
its present value!

In recent times, very large prices have been paid for good
eighteenth-century French furniture. A small Louis XV table
(height 27 inches, length 32 inches) brought $71,000 at the
Gary sale in 1928. A small Louis XVI *secrétaire* fetched
nearly $40,000 at the Rothschild sale in 1937, when prices

were very much depressed. It should be noted that eighteenth-century English furniture has brought prices nearly as high.

Are these prices sound or are they based on false premises? I believe they are sound. A piece of furniture can be a great work of art and may command a high price.

Many people are not aware that furniture can be of great artistic importance. The throngs of visitors to the Wallace Collection in London gaze reverently at the pictures in some of the rooms and hardly glance at the furniture. Yet the furniture is sometimes worth more than the paintings.

Attempts to imitate great eighteenth-century furniture have been made during the nineteenth and early twentieth centuries. Since the First World War began, the wages of skilled labor have been too high to permit such attempts. The best imitations were made by Dasson and Beurdeley in Paris between 1860 and 1890. Their imitations are hard to distinguish from the genuine because they were made with the same materials and tools. There was no profit, however, in producing these almost perfect imitations. The standards of workmanship and material were so high that the imitations sometimes cost more than the originals would have fetched at auction. The Wallace Collection has a replica by Dasson of the famous "Bureau du Roi" by Oeben and Riesener. The replica was two years in the making, and the out-of-pocket cost to Dasson was about 50,000 francs—or $10,000. Beurdeley's commodes are top quality and rarely recognized or identified as copies.

Common imitations of eighteenth-century furniture can generally be told at first glance by an expert. The wood is not old wood; the mounts are electroplated instead of mercury gilded; the chasing is shallow and mechanical—the whole thing simply does not look right.

Once I had gained a fairly sound basic knowledge of the field, I began actively collecting eighteenth-century French furniture. Luck has been with me over the years, and I have succeeded in assembling a collection of which I am rather proud. Since the comment has been widely publicized, I feel that I can quote without compunction or undue immodesty the opinion once expressed by Sir James Mann, director of the Wallace Collection.

"We believe our collection of French eighteenth-century

furniture is the finest in the world," Sir James told author
Ralph Hewins. "Paul Getty's is second. The Louvre ranks
third."

It is difficult—indeed, impossible—to convey in words the
drama, adventure and thrills one experiences when one suc-
ceeds in acquiring a superb chair, divan, desk or other piece
of furniture that is not only an outstanding work of art, but
was also once owned or used by a King of France, a Marie
Antoinette or a Pompadour. Believe me, history and its great
figures do come to life!

When I had well and truly started collecting eighteenth-
century French furniture, my attention was drawn to yet another art form—one apt to be more familiar as such to most
people—namely tapestries. Here I learned that aside from
ancient tapestry, of which we know very little, the history of
tapestry making is divided into four periods: Gothic, Renaissance, eighteenth century and modern.

The best Gothic tapestries were produced by Flemish
weavers between 1475 and 1515, and the supremacy of
these masterpieces of the weaver's art is challenged only by
the best Beauvais and Gobelins tapestries of the eighteenth
century. After 1515, Gothic tapestries became unfashionable
and remained so until the last half of the nineteenth century.
They were replaced by tapestries of Renaissance design, and
these became so popular during the last half of the sixteenth
century that tapestry weaving was one of the major industries
of Flanders.

Louis XIV determined to make France the center of the
tapestry world and, with his usual thoroughness and prodi-
gal expenditure, he succeeded in doing so. He founded the
Gobelins tapestry manufactory in 1662 and the Beauvais in
1664. He brought the best weavers from Flanders to work
the looms and instruct the apprentices and employed the
best French artists to design the "cartoons"—the full-size
studies that served as the models for the weavers to copy in
tapestry.

The Gobelins produced its finest tapestries during the reign
of Louis XIV, although the products of the reigns of Louis
XV and XVI are scarcely inferior. I have been extremely
fortunate to obtain Gobelins specimens for my collection, a

notable example being an 11'2" by 8'8" piece which was woven originally for Chancellor Chauvelin between 1728 and 1730.

It was at Beauvais, however, that the finest tapestries of the eighteenth century were woven. François Boucher made his first cartoons for the Beauvais works in 1735 with a set of fourteen romantic country scenes called *The Italian Fêtes.* These were very popular and, in 1741, Boucher designed another set called *The Story of Psyche* after the fables of Jean de La Fontaine. This series is a masterpiece of Rococo art.

Boucher was advised by his friend Bachaumont to "read and read again the *Psyche* of La Fontaine and, above all things, study Madame Boucher." The artist's wife had posed as a shepherdess in *The Italian Fêtes;* now she became the immortal Psyche. The designs breathe the very spirit of the Rococo—the luxury and loveliness of the best of the eighteenth century. This set, which went on the looms in 1741, continued to be woven until 1770 and gave Boucher first place among tapestry designers. (By a unique stroke of luck, I succeeded in obtaining four of the five magnificent panels for my collection in the 1930s. Among the other Boucher Beauvais examples I have been fortunate enough to purchase are two of the panels from *The Italian Fêtes* and four of the nine panels from the later Boucher work, *The Amours of the Gods.*)

Boucher Beauvais tapestries are, except for a few Gothic masterpieces, the most costly of all tapestries. The Huntington Collection in Pasadena, California, has five panels of *The Noble Pastorale* set, for which Mr. Huntington paid half a million dollars in the late 1920s. Mrs. Hamilton Rice had a complete set of the *Psyche* series of five tapestries, for which she paid $750,000 shortly after the First World War. The set was bequeathed by her to the Philadelphia Museum. One tapestry containing two scenes from *The Amours of the Gods* was sold in New York City in the 1920s for $200,000. (During the depression, I was able to buy it for a fraction of that amount.)

The Rococo mood was best suited to tapestry designs and the New Classicism of the reign of Louis XVI produced tapestries which are less attractive to modern taste. But there is a rich beauty and romantic association about tapestries that even the best pictures somehow cannot equal.

Tapestries, too, bring the past to life the moment one looks at them. They are almost awesome in their fabulous workmanship, their breathtaking beauty and the virtually microscopic detail work of the master weaver's art.

But I have gone far enough afield. It is not my intent to ride any of my personal hobbyhorses to the reader's exhaustion. My purpose has been to skim the surface, sketch in a few bits of colorful background and, perhaps, demonstrate more clearly how extracurricular activities can—and do—capture the imagination, breed broader interests. I've also hoped to show how, as a person becomes more deeply involved in an outside pursuit, so do his enthusiasms grow and the returns he receives in enjoyment and gratification increase.

There is one more point I would like to make, however. For the collector, very often the greatest pleasure of all derives from sharing his enjoyment and gratification with others. Most collectors are not content merely to acquire, to have and hold for themselves, their own private benefit. Appreciating the beauty of the objects they possess, collectors are usually willing—even eager—for others to see, savor and share. That is why they give or loan their finest acquisitions to public museums or establish museums which are open to the public.*

* EDITOR'S NOTE: Mr. Getty is certainly no exception to this rule. Several of the finest pieces from his collection have been donated to the Los Angeles County Museum. Among them are: Rembrandt's "Portrait of Marten Looten"; the famed Ardabil carpet valued at one million dollars; many of the Boucher Beauvais tapestries he has described and several other priceless items. In addition, the bulk of his multimillion-dollar collection has been turned over to the J. Paul Getty Museum, which the author established and maintains in Malibu, California. There, amidst the palatial surroundings Mr. Getty has provided for the treasures, the public may view—without charge—one of America's greatest contemporary collections of fine art. The museum includes the famed Louis XV and Louis XVI galleries that house his collection of eighteenth-century French furniture. There are also Boucher tapestries, Greek marbles from the fabled Elgin Collection, the Lansdowne "Hercules," terra cottas, bronzes and Roman portraits. The picture galleries display works by such great masters as Tintoretto, Titian, Lotto, Gainsborough, Rubens and many others.

Such, in brief, is the story of how a pastime that had its faltering start with a few insignificant purchases made more than half a century ago in the Orient eventually grew and expanded. The efforts expended and the results obtained have been all the more gratifying because I can think that they have made a positive contribution to the American cultural scene and that my collection is now bringing pleasure to others as well as to myself.

As I was careful to preface my discourse, I am making no attempt to proselytize, to convince any of my readers that collecting fine art is *the* or a *must* interest and pursuit for anyone and everyone. I readily acknowledge that it is not to every taste. But please note that I do not say taste *and pocketbook*. For if someone *does* desire to possess works of fine art, he or she can certainly do so nowadays without overstraining the budget or wrecking the bank account.

Although they may not be rare masterpieces of museum quality, there are examples of very good art, indeed, aplenty on the market—and at prices within the reach of today's mechanics and machine-tool operators, schoolteachers and secretaries. Almost anyone who earns even the current average hourly industrial wage can afford *some* type of fine art—and it should be remembered that taste, discrimination and appreciation of beauty and of aesthetic values count for more than money when it comes to "buying art."

In all events, whatever an individual's occupation or profession, and in whatever directions his or her tastes may lie, it remains that no one should "live by work alone." People need to develop interests and pursue activities which are aside and apart from their jobs and provide relaxing and refreshing contrast to the work they perform daily in order to earn their livelihoods.

These leisure-time activities can, I repeat, take any—or preferably many—forms. Golf or gardening, handball or handicrafts, listening to music or learning Magyar, solving community problems or solving crossword puzzles—the "activities mix" depends principally on personal inclination or even idiosyncrasy. The ideal combination, I would hazard to suggest, would be one containing ingredients that provide intellectual, physical, emotional and cultural benefits to the individual.

On the other hand, as long as a person chooses pastimes, avocations, pursuits or hobbies he genuinely likes, engages in them with enthusiasm and gains true satisfaction and enjoyment from or through them, then they are "right" for the individual. The broader the spectrum of his interests, the broader and more tolerant will be his outlook, the more he will be able to understand and appreciate all that is around him—and the closer he will come to being a "connoisseur of life."

I honestly do not feel it in exaggeration to say that extracurricular interests are extrapowerful invigorators. They take years off a person's "age" even while they add years—and spice as well as serenity—to his or her life.

Also, such pursuits are of incalculable value and importance when a human being approaches middle age and the time for retirement from work draws near or arrives.

They go far toward helping one make the psychological preparations for and adjustments to the new situations and conditions, and they aid greatly in avoiding the psychological pitfalls that are frequently the concomitants of these "middle age" and "retirement" milestones in one's life.

11 PSYCHOLOGICAL PREPARATIONS AND PITFALLS

Many people live in apprehensive fear of "middle age" and especially of retirement. Unless adequate psychological preparations are made, the advent of either or both can cause negative—even tragic—results. However, it is not difficult for any intelligent person to make the necessary psychological preparations and avoid the hidden pitfalls. Four simple points that should be taken into consideration to help solve the dilemmas. The plain fact that retirement is a boon—one that opens wide the doors on a wonderful period of complete personal freedom.

It has been remarked that, while very few people travel entirely safe, secure an dcertain paths during their active working careers, for many the greatest crises of uncertainty and anxiety come when they arrive at the crucial crossroads of retirement. Not long ago, a widely syndicated newspaper article quoted a letter to the editor which, in seriocomic vein, gave dramatic emphasis to the psychological problems that may arise.

"This crazy business of getting ready to retire is worse than getting married!" the letter said in part. "Forty-two years ago, I was in a state of dazed confusion as my marriage day approached. But today, with my retirement only months away,

I am even more confused, more unsure of myself, more nervous facing a future I dread. . . ."

According to authoritative sources, the phenomenon is far from unfamiliar—so much so that it has been given a number of popular labels, among them: "middle-age panic," "pre- and postretirement 'jitters'" and "retirement trauma." And there are psychologists, sociologists and physicians who argue persuasively that the melancholia and dread these reactions engender are important factors contributing to such statistical abominations as these:

- The alcoholism rate among people in the 40-to-60 age bracket is reported to be 50 percent higher than that for persons whose ages range from 30 to 39.
- The suicide rate among people over 55 is said to be four times that noted among individuals in the 25-to-34 age group.

If these things are true—and there seems to be no valid reason for doubting the weight of expert testimony on the score—then one is moved to feel dismayed horror by the grim panorama of utterly needless human frustrations, fears and tragedy that presents itself.

Yes, I say and underscore *"utterly needless,"* for there are no supportable grounds why human beings should view middle age or retirement as a bugaboo, bane or as the cemeteries for their hopes, ambitions and capacity for enjoying life. But, before proceeding further, perhaps it would be wise to backtrack a short distance and establish a clear basis on which to build a logical argument.

To begin with, we should accept that in the present context people may be said to fall into one or another of two broad categories. The first, and smaller, segment is comprised of self-employed individuals; the second—and by far the larger —consists of employees.

Now, self-employed persons—doctors, lawyers, owners of business enterprises and so on—enjoy a considerable degree of latitude in deciding the "when" of their retirement. All other things being equal, the self-employed individual may (or *must*) make his own decision regarding the point or age at which he will terminate his active professional or business career.

Not so the employee, the person who works for other individuals, for companies or organizations, government agencies, etc. Be he or she clerk or executive vice-president, in most instances the employee faces the eventuality of an arbitrary age ceiling, upon reaching which retirement is compulsory. The requirement has absolutely nothing to do with the individual's mental or physical capacities; in the majority of cases, it is a must, and there are neither appeals nor extensions.

Whether this is fair and just in individual cases is, at best, a moot question. However, it is the only practicable formula thus far devised for establishing a criterion that is fair, just and equitable to the majority, that does not permit of favoritism and is not harmful to overall employee morale.

If I had it my way, a paramount truth would be drummed into the head of every single employee from the instant he first goes on a payroll: Retirement is neither punishment nor penalty; it is a reward conferred for good and faithful service. Compulsory retirement upon reaching a set age limit does not imply that an individual has outlived his usefulness or has become obsolete. There is no onus attached.

I myself know of numberless people, male and female, who, although they are in their seventies or even older, are at least as competent to do their accustomed jobs as many individuals half their age. But to keep them on a company payroll would be tantamount to instituting a policy of *selective* retirement—and this would lead to suspicions, if not the actual fact, of favoritism. The net result would be serious damage to the morale of all employees—loss of their legitimate hopes and expectations for promotions and advancement within the organization, diminution of their interest and drive and thus dangerous loss of group efficiency.

Withal, as a consequence of compulsory retirement policies, most employees know that when they reach whatever may be the arbitrary "ceiling" age, they must leave their jobs, stepping aside to give other, younger people their chance. How a person accepts this inevitable, adjusts to it, the psychological preparations he makes, the attitudes and plans he forms and formulates against the arrival of "R day" are all crucial factors—throughout his active career as well as after.

Understandably enough, the prospect of eventual retirement does not loom as much of a problem early in the average person's career. The day is too distant and if he thinks of it at all much before the age of forty or so it is, more likely than not, with eager anticipation.

"It will be great to reach the point where I won't have to work anymore!" he very probably tells himself. "Life will be just one long vacation. . . ."

With the passage of years, the outlook most often undergoes a radical change. The maturing individual, who has become interested in his work and accustomed to performing useful, constructive tasks (and who, usually, has received recognition and promotion for his contributions), is now increasingly beset by doubts, fears and uncertainties concerning his retirement.

"What on earth will I do with my time after I retire?"

"How will I be able to reorientate my entire life when I no longer have a job, when I no longer need to assume responsibilities and carry out duties?"

These are the kinds of questions many people begin to ask themselves when they reach their late forties and early fifties. Some are sufficiently realistic and farsighted to arrive at satisfactory answers and even to make comprehensive plans for their postretirement life and activities long before the advent of "R day." Others are not quite so prescient, but nonetheless manage to find entirely adequate solutions for the problem after they have actually retired. Yet others—tragically, far too many of them, if widely publicized reports are to be believed —do nothing but allow their anxieties to grow and intensify until they are finally caught in a trap of despond and despair.

During the next twelve months, more than one million American men and women will reach 65—the age at which, generally speaking, common consent and current usage decree mandatory retirement for most employees. Stated another way, on each and every day of the coming year, a statistical average of some thousands of people in the United States will arrive at what I have called the crucial crossroads of retirement.

How many of them will be psychologically prepared to meet the event with equanimity and to face the future that will follow with delight instead of "dread"?

The question is rhetorical; there are no means whereby one can ascertain or estimate. The answer should, of course, be all—or, at the very least, the overwhelming majority—of those who retire. Certainly, it would seem that people with a modicum of intelligence and common sense should be able to look and plan ahead and begin the necessary process of psychological conditioning well in advance. It strikes me that the process is neither complex nor esoteric—in fact, it should be as simple as the following steps:

1. All who work for a living—be they employees or self-employed persons—should realize very early in their careers that, eventually and inevitably, they must one day retire from their jobs or work. As has been remarked, in the case of employees the *when* of retirement is usually predictable.

2. Employees need to understand clearly that compulsory retirement for age does not stigmatize them as discards and that they have a long and potentially very fruitful and gratifying life ahead of them after they enter the "middle-age zone" and retire from their jobs.

3. The individual who knows when he will retire—after so many years of service or upon reaching a certain chronological age—should set and define the goals he desires to achieve in the interim and thenceforth work energetically and enthusiastically to achieve them.

4. Then he should seek to define—in flexible terms, for his ideas may change—what he desires to do or hopes to accomplish *after* retirement. Whatever thought and planning he devotes to outlining the postretirement program will pay rich dividends.

These four simple steps can do much in advance to resolve the psychological equivalent of what, in physics, has been called "horror vacui"—nature's "dread" of a vacuum. The key elements in the four-step formula are the denial that there will be any "vacuum" after retirement and the affirmation that there will be much to take the place of whatever may be removed or surrendered.

The first two steps help eliminate the fears and anxieties which, psychiatric authorities maintain, lead to melancholia and frustration, despond and deep-seated panic. The third step aids the individual to continue functioning at maximum efficiency, to work and live with definite aim and purpose right up to the day he must leave the XYZ Company's employ. The fourth step (and the sum total of all) ensures that whatever may be "lost" upon retirement will be fully and immediately replaced.

But the skeleton of the foregoing "formula" needs to be fleshed out; the points made will carry much more meaning if they are elaborated upon and given added dimension.

For example, people should recognize that retirement ushers in a period of personal freedom such as they have not known since the day they first began to work—or, perhaps, even since they started attending school.

When an individual retires, his time—a precious commodity on a large part of which there has been a first mortgage for decades—is at last again all his own. The mortgage has been paid in full, and he possesses clear and unencumbered title to 24 hours in every day. The hours and the days are his to do with as he pleases—or as pleases him.

Here, obviously, lies the major rub for those who arrive at the crossroads without adequate psychological preparation. Instead of making full and gratifying use of their time, they succumb to listless boredom or frustrated desperation. They feel that they have been flung onto the junk pile of life—and, what is far worse, they feel sorry for themselves.

Again, needless—and ridiculous—for retirement does not mean an end, but rather a new beginning.

What does the individual want to do after he retires?

Does he want to continue working, either full- or part-time, or start his own business? Or would he rather engage in such enterprises as community projects? Perhaps he'd rather devote himself to leisure activities. Or maybe— But then, the questions will come by themselves, and the answers will follow after thought and reflection, self-examination and self-assessment.

One of the more frequently cited fears of persons facing

retirement is that, after having spent many years working at their trade or profession, they will be unable to continue. The abrupt halt looms, many say, as a terrifying ego-destroying prospect.

"If I have to stop working and earning completely, I'll be like a drug addict given the 'cold turkey' treatment. I don't think I'll be able to take it," one man with an acute case of "preretirement 'jitters'" was recently quoted as telling members of a psychological survey team.

But retirement does not necessarily mean the end of any person's active, income-producing career. Countless individuals, retiring after decades of useful service as employees, go blithely ahead and continue to work productively. They start their own business enterprises; obtain full- or part-time jobs; or use their accumulated knowledge, experience and ability profitably on free-lance, advisory, consultant or kindred bases.

There are considerably more such enterprising men and women than might be imagined. They range from accountants who, after retiring, do free-lance work for small firms or prepare income tax returns for individuals, through mechanics who quickly build up a thriving private trade, all the way, it may be presumed, to zoologists who retire from colleges and universities and write books or give lectures.

One man I know—and he is hardly unique—had a fine work record and held a responsible position with a large manufacturing company. Instead of being dejected or feeling "lost" after his retirement, he joyously celebrated the occasion and announced it signaled the start of a new career.

"I gained plenty of knowledge and experience while working for others. In a manner of speaking, I can even think that all the time I spent as an employee was a sort of on-the-job training period," he declared. "Now, with my savings and retirement benefits, I'll be able to go into business for myself. I can't miss!"

And he didn't miss, either. Starting a business which in no way competed with that of his former employers, he prospered. Within two years, profits proved to be greater by half than the highest salary he'd received as an employee. The hypercritical may argue that this man should have gone into business for himself much earlier, but this is immaterial. The point is that, having retired, he refused to fold up his productive tents. He wanted to keep on working and earning—and did.

A somewhat different example is provided by a much-decorated colonel who, in 1959, retired from the army after completing 30 years' service in the infantry. Although offered a choice of several good positions in private industry, he preferred to return to his medium-sized home town in the Midwest, where, he had long felt, there was much for him to do.

In his blunt infantryman's words, the town was "a damned disgrace." Its public library was a crumbling shell housing a pathetic collection of books. There was no public swimming pool; school gymnasiums were squalid structures without adequate athletic equipment. There were no recreation centers for the community's youngsters—who consequently spent their spare time loafing on street corners or in pool halls.

The colonel chose to make the correction of each of these lacks and deficiencies a personal project. No, he did not run for mayor or even seek a seat on the city council. He was determined to "wake up the people in my home town"—but in his own way and as a private citizen. He and his family had barely settled down to civilian living before he launched a campaign to nudge, prod and shake the town out of its lethargy.

"First, people called me a pest. Then they said I was a nut. At last, folks began to see the light," he recalls.

The veteran officer slowly gained support for his "projects," but more than five years were needed before he attained all his objectives. The final results: a new and well-stocked city library; a large public swimming pool; renovated and re-equipped gymnasiums; a recreation center for youngsters—and, in 1965, a banquet and special award tendered the ex-colonel by his now wide-awake grateful fellow citizens.

Examples reflecting every conceivable form of gratifying postretirement activity and interest are legion, but it hardly seems necessary to list more of them here. A large number and variety have already been cited in earlier chapters. All the individuals concerned have a quality in common; they have learned how to live life to the utmost. Their fundamental philosophy is mirrored in the statement made by the late Charles F. Kettering in 1947, when it was announced that he was retiring as head of the General Motors research department.

"Retirement?" Kettering snorted. "I wouldn't want to fool around with that sort of thing. There's still too much to be done."

For years afterward, he continued to do research work at the Kettering Foundation and in the laboratories of his Foundation for the Study of Chlorophyll and Photosynthesis at Antioch College in Ohio.

Charles Kettering and all the numberless others who have determined to "keep the ball in play" could—and will—never fall prey to "middle-age panic," "pre- or postretirement 'jitters' " or "retirement trauma."

Unquestionably, the surest and safest guarantee against contracting such maladies of mind and emotions is by early self-immunization against their contagion. The individual who prepares himself psychologically, ensuring that no sudden vacuums will develop when he reaches the crucial crossroads, will suffer no shocks or bruises when he encounters the situations and challenges to be encountered there.

Nevertheless, all hope is not lost for even those who fail to take advance precautions or follow the common-sense and eminently practical prescriptions for self-administered preventive medication. There are cures for the afflicted—if they have the clarity of vision to see them or are willing to look, listen and follow instructions when they are brought to their attention.

One—literal—form of treatment is provided by psychiatrists and psychotherapy. Apart from saying that I have heard of countless instances in which these apparently obtained excellent results, I do not believe myself professionally qualified to make comments or state opinions on any matters pertaining to this highly specialized realm of science.

On the other hand, an account of the practical, applied psychology employed by one medical doctor might bear repeating. The physician practices in an area which has a very high ratio of retired folk among its residents. As a consequence, he has a correspondingly high proportion of "senior citizens" among his patients. As might be expected, they very often come to him complaining of a wide variety of aches, pains and infirmities—some real, some imagined. If he is certain the complaints are of the second type, the doctor skillfully guides the ensuing conversation until the patient admits he feels lost, bewildered, unwanted and useless—something that happens very often.

"What do you do all day?" the physician asks at this juncture.

"Not much, I guess," is the gist of the usual reply.

"Isn't that a shameful waste? Think back a few years. Weren't there many things you intended, wanted or hoped to do if you ever had the time?"

Apparently, on some occasions at least, the doctor's patients then and there realize they could be keeping busy—and enjoying themselves—by satisfying long-deferred desires. In other instances, more visits are needed before the dawn breaks. In yet others, all the physician's efforts to revitalize dormant or forgotten interests are without avail.

Speaking strictly as a layman, I consider the underlying principle sound. It seems good practical therapy to encourage people who are dismayed by retirement to do things they'd put off for years because they were occupied—or preoccupied —with work, children, bills and a host of other immediate and pressing problems.

Another among the remedies frequently prescribed for the despondent and disoriented among our retired senior citizens is the miracle analeptic of contact and interaction with other people. The potency of this "treatment" should be self-evident. However, if proof of its efficacy and popularity were needed, it could be found in the thriving "retirement cities" that have sprung up from coast to coast in recent years.

But this is only a single aspect of the multifaceted subject of human relationships and interrelationships and their influence on life and living; it demands to be examined within the context of the whole.

12 THE PLUS AND MINUS OF PEOPLE

"Man," as Seneca said, "is a social animal." The vast majority of human beings need to have social intercourse and to interact with other human beings. But only a foolish person makes "friends" indiscriminately. In order for human relationships to work, certain fundamentals must be borne in mind and followed. One shrewd and sagacious man's classification of people into nine categories. Some of the people-to-people relationship problems that are to be encountered in our present-day, complex society—and a few suggestions for solving them.

Southern California, as most of the world knows, is the land of bright sunshine, quaint and colorful characters—and Japanese gardeners with miraculous green thumbs, one of whom tended the grounds of my Malibu home some years ago.

I am sure that Ito could have grown shamrocks in the Sahara or coaxed marigolds to sprout from marble slabs. However, this is not why I remember him so fondly and well; it is for his wry, dry, all-purpose explanation of the reasons behind humanity's trials and tribulations. To discuss wars or rumors of wars, revolutions, social or economic upheavals or any other critical current events with Ito was to elicit a reply that never varied, even unto his rendering of *l*'s as *r*'s.

"What you expect?" he'd declare with all the solemnity of a Supreme Court Chief Justice delivering a major decision. "People make people. People make world. If enough people crazy, they make everybody and whole world crazy, too."

Oddly enough, although Ito doubtless had no inkling of it and his conclusions were at best oversimplifications of highly dubious merit, his fundamental reasoning closely paralleled that of the most learned and respected sociologists. These scholars hold that the traits and qualities which set man apart from other living creatures have their origins in, are developed by and manifest themselves through social intercourse.

In his posthumously published work *Mind, Self and Society*, the American philosopher George Herbert Mead wrote:

"The self, as that which can be object to itself, is essentially a social structure, and it arises in social experience."

Stated in less ponderous terms, Mead's argument is that human beings are largely what their social contacts and environment make them. Of course, people vary in their capacities to think, learn and perceive; in the ways in which they respond and react to given situations and in many other specifics and details. But, once the necessary qualifying allowances are made, the proposition stands up well. As a superficial but nonetheless valid illustrative example, individuals do not invent their own language or basic manners and mores; they learn and assume those of their society, learning and acquiring them from other members of that society.

Delving deeper into the subject even while he fine-focuses on the individual, sociologist Kingsley Davis, in his book *Human Society*, says:

"No sharp line can be drawn between our own selves and the selves of others, since our own selves function in our experience only insofar as the selves of others function in our experience also."

The sentence, it must be admitted, is recondite, a bit difficult to grasp at first reading. However, Davis is simply emphasizing that no matter how independent and self-sufficient a person may think himself, he nonetheless remains both product of, and contributing participant in, the dynamics of the patterns of social intercourse—of human and group interaction.

A human being is not born with a sense of identity, of self, of being a separate entity. The awareness does not begin to emerge until a child is about two years old; it is only then that he begins to think of himself in terms of pronouns—"I," "me," "mine." He starts using them in speech and distinguishes himself from, say, his mother by calling her "you," in place of the impersonal "mama," which carries no connotations of separate identity of the mother as another self. Students of human behavior maintain that even these first dawnings of awareness are produced to a great extent by the social intercourse of the child with parents, siblings, relatives, nurses and other persons.

The child's sense of being a separate human entity develops with increasing social contact and interaction with other persons until the concept of his own self, as apart from but still having a relation to other separate selves is clearly formed.

Human "selves"—to concoct a rather shaky, spur-of-the-moment simile—may be broadly likened to mirrors which face each other, reflecting and rereflecting both their images. (Needless to say, with humans the "images" neither remain static and unchanging for as long as the "mirrors" of the selves remain facing, nor do they vanish instantly and completely when and if the "selves" are moved apart so that they are not directly facing each other.)

People's egos, their selves and their awareness of being separate entities function only in that and as they "reflect" and are "reflected by" those of others through social intercourse and human interaction. Beyond this, it is through social intercourse and contact that the ego, the self, establishes a value to itself. Kingsley Davis describes the process thusly:

"Since it is built out of the attitudes of others, the self cannot help but place a value on these attitudes apart from or in spite of organic satisfaction. This is especially true of one kind of attitude—the attitude of approval and disapproval, for this offers a key to much else. It is only through the approval of others that the self can tolerate the self."

We seem to have traveled a great distance from our original starting point, but, in fact, we are really not very far from the three-word heart of my erstwhile gardener Ito's catchall philosophy: "People make people."

People *do* "make" people—and, what is more, they have an immensely deep need for each other. Save, perhaps, for the eccentric recluse, fanatic anchorite and phobic misanthrope, people require contact and interaction with—and the approval of—other human beings.

The foundation stones of the self as it is a "social structure" that "arises in social experience" and is "built out of the attitudes of others" are laid at a tender age by the individual's preschool contacts with other people—which contacts are, of course, chiefly within the family group. Thereafter, the individual's circle of acquaintance steadily widens. The "structure" of the self is gradually formed and fabricated as the building blocks of increasing social intercourse and experience are added by contact and interaction with schoolmates, fellow workers and other persons.

Throughout the entire developmental process, the self seeks acceptance and approval by others. The precise forms the individual hopes to have these ends take and the means he employs to attain them are subject to and defined by the capacities, limitations and idiosyncrasies of his intellectual, psychological and emotional equipment.

For example, the well-adjusted and balanced person's efforts to gain acceptance and approbation will follow courses and patterns which, although not necessarily conventional or conformist, are nonetheless socially constructive or, at the very minimum, innoxious. On the other hand, the maladjusted, emotionally frustrated and thwarted individual may—and very often does—resort to distorted or even socially hostile behavior to express himself and draw attention to himself. The attention he receives—be it derision, censure, contempt or even hatred—provides a warped and bizarre form of compensation for the approval that eludes him.

"Notice me. Recognize and acknowledge that I *am* a separate human entity," the juvenile delinquent or aberrant adult is, in effect, pleading. "Give me thereby what I so desperately need—the reassurance that I, too, have an identity and am a 'self' functioning in the experience of other selves."

But then, the essence of the theories and conclusions presented in such meticulously reasoned and documented detail by modern-day scholars was perceived by the ancients. Already, in the first century A.D., the Roman philosopher-statesman Lucius Annaeus Seneca had recognized—and averred—that "Man is a social animal."

Seneca's words, valid as they were in his own time, have gained immense added significance and cogency over the intervening 1,900 years. People today are "social animals" to a far greater degree than their ancestors. No, I do not contend that some freakish biological mutation has radically magnified man's innate gregarious instinct in the short (by evolutionary time scales) period of nineteen centuries. It would be my guess that the *instinct* itself has changed but little since Seneca's day.

The radical alteration is not in the intuitive propensity, but a phenomenon caused by external and environmental pressures. Soaring populations (and, more particularly, population *densities*), the awesome complexity of our contemporary civilization, modern communications miracles and the character of our economic system are some of the forces responsible. These and other factors have compelled enormous increases in the depth, breadth and dynamics of human interdependence and interaction.

Our present civilization is not notably tolerant toward anything remotely resembling a solitary life. It demands many and frequent contacts between people and requires that they interact in most spheres of human activity and at almost all levels of our society.

The person or family living in an isolated house, many miles from the nearest neighbor and without any form of communication with the outside world is a casebook rarity. Nowadays, people live in neighborhoods or in apartment houses—and hold block parties, sign petitions demanding street repairs or form tenants' committees to protest the derelictions of the building superintendent or the landlord.

The jack-of-all-trades farmer who butchered his own cattle, cured their hides and made shoes for himself and his family is but a legend—and a rapidly fading legend at that. Today scores—conceivably hundreds—of people are directly or indirectly involved in the various processes of raising cattle, butchering the animals, tanning their hides, rough-cutting the leather, making shoes and seeing to it that they reach the people who will ultimately wear them.

Where is the owner-operated general store? Even smaller towns have department stores or shopping centers. The housewife with half a dozen items on her shopping list is more than likely to deal with almost as many different sales clerks before she has made all her purchases.

At work—be it in factory, shop or office—the rules call for teamwork, for planned and coordinated group action. Isolationists—even if they call themselves virtuosos—only disrupt the tempo and interfere with the smooth and ordered flow of the work at hand.

Interaction in commerce and industry may or may not be purely or directly business-oriented. As examples, employees of organizations are free to decide whether or not they wish to join company-sponsored social and recreational clubs while, on the other hand, many workers *must* join labor unions. Executive personnel are often tacitly required to become members of country clubs; and of course, in many instances, it is company policy that they perform much of their work through committees.

So much for the work sphere; let us move away from it into the realm of people's private lives. Here, affluence has given people added opportunity to be very active social animals indeed. They give and go to dinner parties, cocktail parties, balls, dances and other social affairs. Clubs and societies of all types flourish. "Little theater" groups, parent-teacher associations, groups organized for special purposes—from supporting charities to taking "package tours" of foreign countries—and myriads of other social groups are bursting at the seams with active members. Fine hotels and caterers are hard pressed to handle all the weddings, debuts, christenings, bar mitzvahs, banquets, school proms and similar events being held these days. (As an aside, I am very aware of this last aspect of the contemporary social picture. The managers of the two luxury hotels controlled by the "Getty interests"—the Pierre in New York City and the Pierre Marques in Acapulco, Mexico—are sometimes at their wits' ends trying to fit "just one more" affair into their jammed schedules.)

Much more could be said on the subject, but I am confident the reader comprehends the necessity for everyday human interaction and is familiar with the accelerated pace of social intercourse—two of the more prominent hallmarks of our time and civilization. And I am equally confident that very few of us would have it any other way.

Most of us are very definitely social animals. We enjoy meeting people and exchanging conversation, ideas and opinions with them; if mutually responsive chords are struck, we relish their company and want to know them better. Whether it is for the psychological "profit" of further building our "selves" out of the attitudes of others or merely for the sheer enjoyment we derive from warm and *simpatico* human contact, we *do* need face-to-face relationships with other people.

Now, when human beings are young, ebullient and quick to generate enthusiasms, they often tend to view and value their relationships with others in quantitative, rather than qualitative, terms. Their criterion is solely how many friends and acquaintances they have, and they give little or no weight to variable factors which could have an extenuating effect on their judgment. There is nothing fundamentally wrong with this; it is just another symptom of what, in my youth, carried the homely label of "growing pains."

Youth thrives on what it calls "popularity." Fortunately, sheer exuberance is a wholly satisfactory interim substitute for the ability to discern and distinguish—an ability acquired only after the requisite quota of disappointments and disillusionments has been experienced.

As the individual matures a bit and gains a better and sounder perspective—not to mention the priceless lessons he learns through receiving a few hard knocks—he begins to measure personal relationships with a qualitative yardstick. If he possesses reasonable intelligence and fair eyesight, he soon makes the discovery we all must inevitably make—that it takes time to form friendships and, conversely, that time is the sole reliable test that tells if friendships are genuine.

The discovery is usually followed by a process of assessment, winnowing, sorting and classifying. For some reason, the English language is sadly deficient in nouns denoting the precise shades and gradations of relations possible between human beings. Hence, most people are forced to devise their own classifications, rating scales and criteria, as well as guides to their attitudes and behavior toward persons in the various categories. A business associate with whom I recently whiled away an hour or so discussing the subject later dictated and sent me his version of a taxonomy of human relationships. Although presented in a droll vein, the criteria, value scales and categories are unquestionably very similar to those the average mature individual formulates for himself:

1. **Pariahs.** Patently inimical, malicious or untrustworthy persons. Treat as if they were carrying bombs with lighted short fuses. Run—do not walk—to the nearest escape hatch to avoid them.

2. **Torments.** People who are antipathetic, chronic and case-hardened bores or just downright unpleasant. Keep all at a respectful distance, but if an encounter with a specimen is inevitable, grit—or show—your teeth and disengage as soon as possible.

3. **Exasperations.** Insipid, dull or mildly irritating—but otherwise comparatively harmless—individuals. Grin and bear it—but only until you find an opportunity to slip the hawser with good grace.

4. **Acquaintances, Mark I.** You don't really know why it is, but when you're in the company of members of this species, you feel restless, strained, uncomfortable. Recommended action: (a) Try to find out why you react the way you do and see if the burr can be taken out from under the saddle; (b) if (a) doesn't work or isn't worth the bother, scratch the people off your list. Who wants to feel restless, strained and uncomfortable?

5. **Acquaintances, Mark II.** Individuals whose company can be pleasant enough, if taken in small quantities and at long intervals. Just make sure you don't increase the dosage or increase the frequency.

6. Acquaintances, Mark III. People with whom you get along well and enjoy yourself—but with whom your relationship is relatively superficial. Unless the relationship grows spontaneously, let it stay as it is; forced feeding might kill it entirely.

7. Counterpoints. Persons with whom you share some common interests and have established a moderate-to-good degree of rapport. Such relationships are rewards in themselves and well worth the effort spent in cultivating them.

8. Odds-on Favorites. These are what, for want of a better term, can be called "probationary friends," or more appropriately, "probationary friendships." Warm amity, mutual understanding, community of interests, mutual regard and respect—in fact, all the elements of genuine friendship save one are there. Still among the missing: the leavening of tests and trials. What to do? Simple, just give it time.

9. True friendships. If you need explanation of this, you have no real friends—and can't be a real friend to anyone!

Had I composed the foregoing scale of human relationships, the wording might have been different, but the principles and conclusions would not have varied from those expressed by its author. True friendships are rare and precious, and the emotionally mature person knows they cannot be made quickly or haphazardly. They begin with correlative processes of selection, take root slowly and develop gradually.

By all logical rights and precedents, the fruits of enduring acquaintanceships and genuine friendships should be at their ripe best when the parties to them reach middle age—and particularly after they retire. It is then that individuals have the unencumbered time and opportunity to share mutual interests, participate in communal activities and otherwise enjoy each other's company to the full. But a strange irony presents itself nowadays. Even as life expectancies have increased and life has become easier, more secure and more affluent for more and more people, so have the probabilities that individuals may keep up their long-standing friendships declined. Behind this paradox lie several major revolutions

that have taken—and are still taking—place in the living pa
terns of our people.

For purposes of illustration, consider the mythical—b
typical—"case histories" of two American family groups. A
though separated in time by only a generation and, in mo
outward respects, almost identical to each other, they migl
have come from two different worlds—which, in more tha
one sense, they do.

First, there are the Martins, John and Marie. Natives of
small upstate New York city, they married in their twentie
and had three children, two sons and a daughter. Joh
worked as a skilled technician in a paper mill and, in 193(
upon reaching the age of 65, retired. John and Marie owne
their own home, and it was the most natural thing that the
should continue to live there, remaining in their familiar su
roundings, among their old friends and close to their childre
and grandchildren, for their sons had made their homes an
careers in the same city, and their daughter had married
"hometown boy."

Now shift attention to Robert and Anne Powell. At th
present time, he is 62; she is 57. They, too, were born an
raised in a small town—say, perhaps, in Michigan. Like th
Martins, the Powells had two sons and a daughter, the:
names and present ages: Charles, 34; Edward, 32; and Eliza
beth, 28. Robert Powell had a job roughly equivalent in na
ture to that held by John Martin, but with a manufacturin
concern, and he also owned his own home.

But here the parallels and resemblances end.

The Powells sent their children to a state university. Whe
Robert retired, his son, Charles, was working for the Unite
States Government—in South America. The second boy, Ec
ward, was employed by an aircraft company in Seattle, Wash
ington. Daughter Elizabeth was married to a young executiv
in a large organization, and based in Baltimore, Maryland.

The senior Powells, having made their plans for "R day
long before, sold their house and moved to the warmer, mor
salubrious climes of Florida, where, with their savings an
Robert's retirement benefits, they were able to live in modes
comfort. Obviously, the Powells left behind old and goo
friends with whom their contacts were thereafter reduced t

exchanging letters or infrequent visits. But they had antici-pated this when making their plans and were thus able to adjust to their new environment without a heavy sense of loss and quickly made fresh acquaintances and began to form new friendships.

These two much-abbreviated "case histories" reflect some of the sharp contrasts between the then and the now of the 'American way of life." Sweeping sociological changes have marked the last few decades at every plane and in every pat-tern of social behavior. The family ties that once served to bind three or even more generations to the geographical lim-its of a city, town or certain rural area have been cut or greatly loosened. People have become freely mobile; they move from one city or state to another with hardly a second thought.

The scale of population shifts is vast. The United States Bureau of the Census has reported that the nation's farm popu-lation is declining at a rate approaching 5 percent per year. The "small town," long the traditional backbone and bulwark—or so some would have it—of American society is virtually a dying institution. The mass exodus from such hamlets to urban areas has added tens of millions to the populations of large metropolitan centers and their suburbs.

Forces and factors such as these are swiftly eroding the once reliable guarantees of close and constant contact with immediate family and long-time friends. This has particular significance and poses special problems for many persons near-ing—or reaching—middle age or the time when they must retire. Individuals whose ideas of postretirement social rela-tionships are based on obsolete concepts need to revise and reorientate their thinking to prevent a sudden "social inter-course vacuum" from developing when their friends and fam-ily move away, or when they move away from friends and family.

Neither I nor anyone else can advise others how to go about making new acquaintances or forming friendships to fill any such vacuum. The means and methods are up to the individual. However, I have observed that, under average circumstances, the average person encounters few difficulties or obstacles in making new acquaintances and forming new friendships as long as he—or she—is willing to give as well as take. Reciprocation is the key, the touchstone. Rarely, if ever, will a scowl bring a smile as a response—and, just as water seeks its own level, people seek other people whose attitudes and interests are similar to their own.

It stands to reason that, whenever and wherever it is practicable, the retired person should exert every effort to maintain old acquaintances and friendships. But by no means should this be the sum and limit. Postretirement is—as I have repeatedly argued or implied—a new and wonderfully free stage in one's life. Among the many previously withheld or severely restricted potentials and opportunities it offers are those for enlarging one's circle of acquaintance and forming new friendships.

Common sense alone tells us that people need people, face-to-face relationships, social intercourse and interaction with others at least as much after retirement as before. The individual who, after retiring, deprives himself or herself of the associations and consociations that add body, zest and spice to life—that, indeed, add the "human" to human activity and existence—is willfully withdrawing from the mainstream of such activity and existence.

Physical health + psychological preparation + activities and interests + gratifying human relationships − pernicious myths and misconceptions × an individual's energy and enthusiasm = the negation of age and triumphant "connoisseurship of life" after retirement.

Such is the gist of the proved formula. However, as given above it lacks the key element of practical considerations—and it is high time that we examine this vital aspect of the issue.

13   A FISCAL PRIMER

Money may not be everything—but it is very important in every-one's life. Luckily, due to social legislation and enlightened pro-grams and policies, fewer and fewer of our people need fear poverty in their later years and after they retire from work. Never-theless, the prudent person looks ahead and seeks to provide a maximum degree of financial security for his later years. Thoughts on how the average individual might go about resolving familiar fiscal problems—and the three initial steps everyone should take to begin proper planning for retirement.

Dollars and cents.

    Pounds, shillings and pence.

Rubles and kopecks.

It doesn't really make a great deal of difference if one lives in a free-enterprise society, a semisocialized welfare state or a communist country. Whatever obfuscations the ideologies of each system advance in efforts to prove otherwise, there are certain immutable economic facts of life that are common to all.

If people are to have food, clothing and other necessities— and comforts and luxuries—they must obtain money with which to buy them. During their active years, most people "obtain" money by earning it through work. And one may generalize that an individual receives material rewards in proportion to the commercial value of the services he renders. This is particularly valid in our free-enterprise system, but it must be remembered that even the Stakhanovite who exceeds his "norms" fares better than the workers who do not.

Now, as a rule, a line charting the course of an individual's earnings starts at a comparatively low point at the beginning of his career and rises over the years as he gains knowledge and experience, performs more important tasks and receives promotions and pay boosts. There are, of course, exceptions. For extreme example, a child motion picture star's income may reach dizzying heights before he is ten, and then, because he loses public favor, plummet to zero and never again be more than a fraction of the amount earned in childhood. Or various factors may cause dips, drops or complete reversals in the upward trend of a person's earnings at any point in his career; however, these are departures from normal patterns.

Thus, it may be further generalized that, as the employee or self-employed person approaches middle age, he also approaches the peak of his earnings. Then he retires, and while his income derived from work ceases, his need to "obtain" money continues. Nowadays, most civilized countries have comprehensive programs and effective machinery to provide their citizens with at least minimal postretirement incomes.

Adverse propaganda to the contrary, the United States is well up among the leaders in taking care of its people and lightening their fears of the future. There exists, within the framework of our robustly functioning free-enterprise system, a broad spectrum of programs and schemes that guarantee Americans they will continue to "obtain" money after retirement. The cornerstone of all these is, of course, the Social Security Act, which was originally passed in 1935 and has since been greatly expanded and amplified.

Almost every employee and self-employed person in the United States is covered by the federally administered Social Security insurance program. Benefits paid out by the Social Security Administration to retired persons, their qualifying survivors and individuals unable to work due to disability total some $20 billion per year. Granted, the individual monthly retirement payments are not prodigal; they do not allow the recipients to bathe in vintage champagne or gorge themselves on caviar. But that has never been the intent of the Social Security program. Its purpose is to provide Americans with a reasonable degree of assurance that their basic needs will be met after they retire or are no longer able to work. And, it should be emphasized, Social Security payments are not gifts; they are insurance benefits accruing from "policies" purchased by the Social Security tax "premiums" collected from employers and employees.

Recent amendments to the Social Security Act provide hospital and medical insurance for retired persons. They also increased the maximum earnings on which retirement benefits may be computed (to $6,600) and augmented the monthly cash benefits.

The table below gives a sampling of the benefits.

Average Yearly Earnings After 1950:	$ 1,800	$ 3,600	$ 4,800	$ 6,600
Disability benefits ⎱ Retirement at 65 ⎰	$ 78.20	$112.40	$135.90	$168.00
Retirement at 64	73.00	105.00	126.90	156.80
Retirement at 63	67.80	97.50	117.80	145.60
Retirement at 62	62.60	90.00	108.80	134.40
Wife's benefit at 65 or with child in her care	39.10	56.20	68.00	84.00
Wife's benefit at 64	35.90	51.60	62.40	77.00
Wife's benefit at 63	32.60	46.90	56.70	70.00
Wife's benefit at 62	29.40	42.20	51.00	63.00
Widow, age 62 or over	64.60	92.80	112.20	138.60
Widow at 60, no child	56.00	80.50	97.30	120.20
Widow, under 62 and one child	117.40	168.60	204.00	252.00
Widow, under 62 and two children	120.00	240.00	306.00	368.00

But Social Security benefits are by no means the only

forms of retirement income known to Americans. Among the
others are: company, union or joint company-union pension
plans; civil service, military service and veterans' pensions
Railroad Retirement Act benefits. And the provident individ
ual can also further guarantee that he will continue to "obtain"
money after retirement. Interest on bank savings, income
from annuity policies purchased from private insurance com
panies and dividends or profits deriving from investments of
various kinds are some of the more common sources.

Withal, it remains that there should be practical, hard-fac
advance planning for retirement—a task each individual mus
undertake personally. No one can prepare the blueprints for
him, because no two individuals or families have identica
preretirement situations or postretirement aims and ambitions
These are subject to an astronomical number of variable fac
tors ranging from individual capabilities—and whims—to to
morrow's unforeseeable developments, which may tip the
scales up for one person and down for the next.

Nevertheless, there are broad, common-sense guidelines
which, after modifying and adapting them to their own par
ticular situations, most people can use as initial reference
points when they begin to rough out their plans for "R day.'
None of the hints and pointers are answers in themselves
they serve merely to pose the questions and problems—and
sometimes the dilemmas—that require decision and resolution
by the individual himself.

First, there is the question of *when* one should begin prac
tical, dollars-and-cents preplanning and programming. The
theoretical optimum is obvious. Suppose, for argument's sake
that a person goes to work at 21 and retires at 65. The forms
and patterns his postretirement life and situation will take and
follow are determined over the intervening 44 years. The far
sighted and provident (but, I fear, extremely rare) individua
would therefore start his practical planning for "R day" upon
receiving his first pay check. Certainly it would be an excellent
idea.

As just one example, since he is only 21, premiums on an
nuity policies maturing at age 65 are very low. A "starter'
policy (which can always be increased later, when he is earn
ing more money) may be purchased for no more than the

cost of a packet of cigarettes a day. Or suppose that during his first year at work, he deposits $52—a dollar each week—into a savings account paying 4.5 percent interest. If he leaves that $52 in the bank, allowing the interest on it to be compounded annually, he will have $360.88 on the day he retires. This last is, of course, a primer-level illustration, but it does dramatically demonstrate that money invested early and wisely has a remarkable propensity for growth over the years.

However, it has been my observation—and, I must ruefully confess, my personal experience—that when one is young, it is almost impossible to conceive of ever reaching middle age. The average person will not—he is constitutionally unable to—begin practical planning for retirement until he becomes consciously aware of the inevitability of retirement. At what age or stage that will happen depends on the individual. In any event, it is never too early to start—but it is never too late, either, for a few years, or even months, of preparation are better than no preparation at all.

The second rule of thumb is that every person must grapple with what is essentially a "peg and hole" problem. It stems from the well-known fact that any number and variety of causes frequently create a feasibility gap—or gulf—separating "want to do" from "able to do." The problem is not only widespread, it may also have far-reaching psychological ramifications and repercussions.

The late Dr. Adolf Meyer, for many years the director of the Henry Phipps Psychiatric Clinic at Johns Hopkins Hospital, once wrote:

The greatest difficulty in life, the greatest source of disharmony, apart from the influences of heredity, infectious disease and poor feeding and poor chances for growth, is the discrepancy between impulse, yearning and ambition on the one hand, and the actual opportunities and the actual efficiency of performance on the other. We all know people who try continually to put square pegs into round holes. They are unwilling or unable to learn to know and accept their own nature and the world as it is and to shape their aims according to their assets.

In a large percentage of cases in which persons come to grief in their mental and moral health, the trouble is of just that kind. Failing with what is frequently impossible and undesirable anyhow, these persons develop emotional attitudes and habits and tendencies to fumble or to brood or to puzzle or to be apprehensive until what students of the functional diseases of the heart call "a break of compensation" occurs, a break of nature's system of maintaining the balance, with a more or less sudden slump and implication of collateral functions.

As a layman, I am usually hesitant to take issue with anyone possessing professional credentials as impressive as those of Dr. Meyer. However, while I find myself in agreement with almost all he says, I must reject the principle of passive surrender and defeatism implicit in the final sentence of the first paragraph quoted. Experience and observation have proved to me that it is not always necessary for people to "shape their aims according to their assets." I offer in rebuttal that many people manage to increase and multiply their "assets" to accommodate their "aims." Granted, it is seldom, if ever, easy—and sometimes it is impossible.

Suppose that Tom Smith wants to make a hobby of skin diving, but physicians bluntly warn him that his heart will not stand up under the strains of the sport. Obviously, Tom must abandon his desire, or, in effect, commit suicide.

Bill Jones would dearly love to run for public office, but he lacks the presence and personality needed to win people's support—and votes. Here, it is conceivable that with great determination and effort, Jones can "remake" or vastly improve himself and the qualities which prevent him from realizing his ambitions.

Don Thompson yearns to take a trip around the world. However, he does not have the assets—in the literal sense of the term—to satisfy the yearning; he simply does not have the money to make the voyage. But who is to say that Don Thompson cannot—or will not—work harder, save more and accumulate sufficient funds to make his dream come true?

One could pose and speculate over an infinity of hypothetical situations that have their counterparts or close parallels in real life. He would unavoidably arrive at the obvious conclusion that human beings are not always able to do or have everything they desire exactly as, if and when they desire it. People often find it necessary to reconcile conflicting quantities and qualities and bridge the feasibility gap by compromising on the best, most viable medium between what they want—or would like—to do and what they are able to do. But, with all due respect to Dr. Meyer, only the most dour pessimist would cling to the dogma that people must invariably and passively "accept their own nature and the world as it is" and "shape their aims according to their assets."

The individual planning ahead for retirement is especially likely to be faced with this problem of fitting the peg of his aspirations to the hole of the attainable. Naturally, when preparations are begun in reasonable time and made with care, the chances are excellent that the hole can be shaped or enlarged to accommodate the peg. Conversely, if planning is delayed overlong or done haphazardly, it is the peg that will have to be modified, by trimming and whittling it down.

The range of activities and interests open to the average retired person and the elements that make for a full and varied life have been discussed already, at some length and in considerable detail. There is no need to make further mention of them here, save to venture the opinion that, with proper planning, the pursuits which bring the individual the most enjoyment and gratification need not be "whittled from the peg."

Whenever it is begun, "proper" practical planning for retirement would seem logically to commence with three initial steps:

1. Broad definition of one's ultimate aims and objectives and intended activities.

2. Rational inventory and appraisal of one's existing resources and realistic estimate of future opportunities for augmenting and enhancing them.

3. If, upon critical scrutiny and evaluation, the sum of the latter is not clearly sufficient to permit full realization of the former, it is for the individual to seek new or more effective means for increasing his resources. With imagination and enterprise, he will find them—and determination and effort will make them produce the desired results.

As has been remarked, each person's preretirement situation is unique unto itself, and hence he must formulate and implement his own decisions and programs. Even so, the example and experiences of others frequently teach lessons, generate ideas and suggest solutions. On these grounds, it might be worthwhile to violate a cardinal rule of good manners and intrude on the privacy and pry into the personal affairs of Carl J. Black.

14 POINTERS FOR PRACTICAL PLANNING

The mythical Mr. Carl J. Black demonstrates some simple and effective means and methods whereby the average person preparing for retirement can start putting his financial house in order years— or even decades—before he retires. The questionnaire Mr. Black prepares for himself—and the simple "financial documents" he and his wife prepare and keep up to date to assure themselves that they will be in the best possible financial condition when retirement becomes a reality.

A fictional character created solely to mime his way through a brief, quasidocumentary drama, Carl J. Black bears resemblance to no real person. Yet he could be any one—or a composite—of countless American males.

Carl Black has just turned 50, enjoys excellent health and is married. His wife, Helen, is 47. The Blacks own their house—subject to mortgage—and have two children, both of whom are fully grown, married and living away from the family home. Carl has worked for the same—and thriving—company for 19 years. His superiors regard him as a fine and valuable employee; hence his job is secure.

These are all the vital statistics available. Carl has been

purposely reduced to bare outlines, for our scenario is, in effect, a preretirement planning primer. As such, its terms must be broad and elastic enough for the moderately apperceptive spectator to translate them easily into his own situational idioms.

However, a few introductory program notes are in order. That Carl Black "has just turned 50" is a relevant detail. Several authoritative sources claim that this is a critical milestone for many, possibly most, American males. They say it is upon reaching the 50-year mark that large numbers of men awaken fully to the inexorable approach of retirement. The impact has been noted to cause psychological and emotional reactions ranging from ebullient delight through depression or panic to "nervous breakdown."

Fifty is also said to be the age when very many men begin full-scale practical planning for retirement. All things considered, it is a propitious time. At 50, the average man is mature, seasoned and in fine physical and mental condition. His career base is likely to be well established and, whether or not through his own conscious, foresighted efforts, quite a few of his preliminary preparations are already made. His Social Security and, frequently, company or union pension plan accounts are growing. Very probably, he has some savings and insurance—and assets and investments, if naught else, in his home.

Yes, by his fiftieth birthday, the average man has a firm foundation laid. And, what is more, he still has an impressive amount of time and opportunity to draw up his detailed blueprints and build further on that foundation before he retires.

Whereupon, we dim the houselights and begin the performance of "Tableaux from the Private Life of Carl J. Black." As the curtain goes up, we find that Carl has definitely decided to retire at 62, twelve years from now. He is pondering how best to begin planning a practical program that will enable him and his wife (it will be recalled that her name is Helen) to fit the hefty peg of their postretirement aspirations into the still appreciably undersized hole of their available and anticipated resources.

Now, we do not know whether Carl Black is an electrician, an engineer or an executive vice president—and we do not really care. For, whatever his occupation, Black demonstrates that he is an eminently well-balanced individual who possesses a large measure of maturity and common sense.

The realization that he is past 50 has not brought on any attacks of "middle-age panic" or "preretirement jitters." Very much to the contrary, Carl is relaxed as he gathers his thoughts. Since he has decided to get down to the business of planning how to make the most of the next dozen years, he reasons that the most efficient way to go about it is in an orderly, businesslike fashion.

Carl Black is well aware that he will need to devote innumerable evening and weekend hours to his task and expend much effort and energy before anything resembling a finished blueprint emerges. However, he tells himself, first things first. He gets up from his easy chair, crosses the room, sits down at his desk, takes pen and paper—and starts to write out a list of questions for himself. He pauses frequently to think, but, after a time, the list is apparently complete. Carl lays down the pen, leans back in his chair and carefully reads over what he has written.

Carl Black's first-step-toward-planning list is arranged in prudent order and goes like this:

A. Wills

1. Do Helen and I both have properly executed, legally valid wills?
2. Are they up to date, containing all and exactly the provisions we wish to make?
3. Are they written so as to take full advantage of all the latest legal and legitimate tax benefits?
4. Note to myself: If there are any doubts, or any changes or additions need to be made, make an appointment with my attorney at the earliest opportunity.

B. Debt Situation

1. Aside from minor current bills, how much do I owe and to whom?

2. Will all my present debts—including the mortgage on the house—be paid off by the time I retire?
3. If the answer to the above is negative, how can I clear all the obligations before the deadline?

C. Insurance

1. Note: Make an appointment with my broker and review my entire insurance situation.
2. What is my life and annuity insurance status?
3. Are the values of the policies I hold sufficient, and will they be paid up by the time I retire?
4. If not, can I afford to increase the policies, or, on the other hand, would I be better off shifting into paid-up policies so there will be no premium payments due after retirement?
5. How do Helen and I stand on health and hospitalization insurance—especially in light of the new Medicare program?
6. Which (if any) of the various policies of all kinds that we now hold can be dropped twelve years from now?
7. What (if any) types of coverage that we do not have now is it advisable for us to obtain in preparation for retirement?

D. Savings

1. Do we have an ample, immediately available "cash cushion" in the form of bank savings?
2. Is the money drawing the maximum interest being paid by federally insured savings institutions?
3. Would it be a wise move to increase the size of the "cushion" by allotting more of my present income to savings?
4. Or, conversely, is the "cushion" showing signs of growing too fat for the purpose it is intended and would it be advisable to shift some of the money into investments paying higher returns?

E. Securities

1. How much do I have invested in government bonds, and what are the maturity dates of the bonds?

2. If all the bonds are "E" Series, would there be advantage to converting any of them into "H" Series bonds—and, if I do switch, what are the deferred income tax possibilities?

3. All facts and figures—present and foreseeable—taken into consideration, should I go even further and use some of the money now tied up in government bonds to purchase other securities offering higher yields or growth possibilities?

4. But then, what is my situation in regard to mutual funds, common-stock holdings and similar investments?

5. Considering that I have twelve active years ahead of me, am I receiving the maximum benefits from the "spare cash" I have invested in mutual funds or common shares?

   Reminder to myself: call my broker for an appointment and talk the entire matter over with him. If possible, try and obtain cross-reading on his advice and forecasts from another reliable source.

F. Real Estate

1. What properties—including the house—do I own and what, if any, are the mortgages on them?

2. What are the fair market values of the properties—and what would be my net proceeds if I sold them or my equities in them?

3. Are any of the properties even now clearly a burdensome liability in that they produce no income, have less value than when I bought them or require unduly high outlays for maintenance, repairs, taxes, etc.?

4. How can I best get out from under the burdens, realize cash from their sale and use the money to better, more profitable advantage?

That is Carl Black's initial checklist, a basic document in what, thereafter, will be a steadily growing file. However, the list itself will keep Carl busy for quite a while. . . .

The curtain is lowered momentarily to denote the passage of the several weeks—or, more probably, months—Carl needs to obtain detailed answers to all the questions and to resolve the problems they pose.

When we see Carl J. Black again, he is once more seated at his desk, a manila folder thick with papers at his elbow and a serenely serious look on his face. His wife, Helen, sits in a chair nearby, calmly knitting, but obviously very much alert and interested in the conversation she is having with her husband.

The replies to the questions on Carl's original list had provided the Blacks with a sharply delineated picture of their situation. Certain imbalances, flaws and weaknesses were revealed—and, as a result, certain adjustments, corrections and improvements have been made. Husband and wife are now able to take another businesslike step in planning for Carl's retirement and realistically draw up some additional vitally important documents.

Carl is working on the first of these—a "balance sheet" reflecting the Blacks' current overall financial condition. Since he wants only a reasonably accurate approximation of their net worth as of the moment, Carl feels free to simplify and improvise. Therefore, he boils his "balance sheet" down to the major essentials of the family's "Assets" and "Liabilities," with the following headings and subheadings:

ASSETS

Current Assets

Cash savings.

Marketable securities, shown at cost, but with current market value noted in parentheses.

Cash or loan value of life, annuity and endowment policies.

"Accounts Receivable" (amounts due from notes or loans, less reasonable provision for loss from bad debts).

Major, nonessential items of personal property readily convertible into cash (for example, stamp or coin collections, etc.) listed at conservatively estimated market values.

Other, or "Long-Term" Assets

(These are assets not very readily convertible into cash or,
usually, real property which, although it may be easily
mortgagable, tends to be "fixed.")

Net realizable value of real property owned outright or of
equity therein.

Net realizable value of leases held.

Net realizable value of all other property or investments not
quickly convertible into cash.

TOTAL ASSETS:

LIABILITIES

Current Liabilities

Major accounts and debts existing as of current date and
payable within the next year.

Estimated federal income taxes accrued to date in excess of
taxes withheld or prepaid.

Estimated state income taxes accrued to date.

Property taxes.

Long-Term Liabilities

Mortgages.

Notes and other obligations due more than a year from current date.

Other long-term debts.

TOTAL LIABILITIES:

By deducting the amount of their *total liabilities* from that
of their *total assets,* the Carl Black family obtains a fair—
though by no means exact—idea of its *net worth.* This indi-
cates whether their fundamental financial condition is sound,
or warns that the underpinnings are shaky or sagging. All in
all, such a "balance sheet" is an invaluable source of infor-

mation and an equally important tool for any family's practical planning.

Carl and Helen Black add up their figures, determine their net worth, and call it a night. They have their son and daughter-in-law over for dinner the following evening and play bridge with friends on the next. It isn't until Saturday afternoon that they can get to work on the second key financial document, an "Income Statement" for the coming year.

This is an educated guess-estimate, but likely to be quite accurate. The Blacks have detailed records of their income and outgo for preceding years, and they can calculate within tolerable limits what Carl's salary and other job income will be. And so he prepares a statement estimating what will be received—and what must be or will be spent—during the coming year. He does it in this manner:

Income

Salary, commissions, etc., after tax withholding and other deductions.
Interest and dividends.
Income from rents and similar sources.
Income from sales of property, etc.
Other income.

TOTAL:

Expenditures

Fixed expenses (mortgage or rent payments, etc.).
Interest payments.
Taxes.
Insurance.
Maintenance and repair of property owned.
Household expenses, including food and utilities, etc.
Clothing.
Automobile expenses.
Miscellaneous (under this heading, Carl lumps everything from entertainment to postage and pocket money).

TOTAL:

The foregoing is loose, even untidy—but nonetheless entirely adequate for the purposes intended. Carl and Helen Black will do their down-to-the-last penny bookkeeping at income tax time. Right now, their interest is limited to estimating how much of a surplus they will have at the end of the following year and, needless to say, in seeing if there are any unwarranted bulges in their list of forecasted expenditures.

When they have a rough idea of the surplus, they can begin thinking of how it should be allocated—how much to be deposited in the savings bank, how much used for buying government bonds and so on. As for the bulges, since they see them on paper before they actually develop into cash-consuming realities, the Blacks can take the necessary preventive measures and trim the fat before it forms.

The curtain drops once again, leaving Carl and Helen to pore over their "Income Statement." It rises on an almost identical scene, but the time is some days or weeks later. The Blacks have just completed the last of their three key financial documents—the least exact of them all. It is merely a rough forecast—and it is done in pencil, for there will be many changes made in it.

The paper is a broad estimate of what the Blacks' income and outgo will be more than a decade later—after Carl has retired. None of the figures shown are reliable, for prices and costs fluctuate, Social Security and pension-plan benefits may be changed overnight—and, for that matter, there is no way of guessing what money will be worth by the time Carl Black's "R day" arrives.

Nevertheless, the forecast will prove a distinct aid to the Blacks in their preretirement planning.

Each year, they will prepare a new balance sheet and income statement. Since they will also keep an eye cocked on price and cost trends—and be aware of any changes in Social Security or pension-plan retirement benefits—they can keep the figures listed on their forecast sheet up to date and by comparing the three documents see clearly how they are progressing toward their goals.

And so, the final curtain is lowered on Carl J. Black and

his wife. He—and she, too, for that matter—can be applauded loudly. They have done very well, creating a sensible basic framework for practical preretirement planning—one that almost anyone of any age can modify and adapt for his own use.

But the drama is not really over; it will continue for years behind the scenes. The final fiscal ending—for the Blacks or for anyone else—is decided by what they actually do with their surplus funds between the day they begin active preparation and the dawn of "R day" itself.

How—and how wisely and well—will they save and invest? There is certainly no shortage of opportunities for doing either or both. Each form—from federally insured savings accounts to common stocks—offers attractions and advantages. And each has its dangers and drawbacks. All bear close examination and study.

15 CLOSER FOCUS ON THE FUTURE

The historical trend of prices is up. The buying power of the dollar is being gradually eroded. There is little indication—or hope— that the trend will change in the foreseeable future. Thus, the individual looking toward his postretirement future should take steps to counteract the erosion of his money. Prudent individuals begin by creating a "cash cushion" of savings that is immediately available in case of emergency, but which still earns some return. Some hints and guides—and a few common-sense warnings.

Mattresses, coffee tins—or, for that matter, safety-deposit boxes—are neither safe nor sane repositories for spare cash. Regardless of how well guarded the mattress, how cleverly concealed the coffee tin or how heavily armored the safety-deposit vault, none of them offers the least degree of protection against the elements that erode the real value of money.

A hundred—or a thousand or a million—dollars squirreled away under the floorboards of a clothes closet ten years ago may still be intact, untouched by pilfering hands. However, whatever the sum, its actual worth has been diminished by the ravages of economic trends just as surely as though a thief had been making periodic raids on the hoard, stealing a little at a time.

In 1967, a dollar buys less than it did in, say, 1957—and the farther one goes back in time to make comparisons, the greater and more glaring is the disparity.

For instance, gauged in terms of purchasing power, today's American dollar is roughly equivalent to:

- Forty cents in 1938–39.
- Twenty-five cents in 1914.

Parenthetically, it might be of interest to note that, in the early sixteenth century, money had *forty times* the buying power that it had in 1914!

Agreed, other economic trends have acted as compensatory forces. Increased wages and salaries—*more* dollars per unit or measure of work—have offset the decline in the real value of the monetary unit itself, to such extent that more people have greater actual buying power now than ever before.

Without inquiring further into the esoterics of economic theory, one may readily postulate that:

1. The established, historically proved economic trend is inflationary, steadily decreasing the purchasing power of the monetary unit even while increasing the supply of money.
2. There are no indications to justify the belief (or hope) that the trend will—or can—change in your lifetime or mine.
3. It is therefore inescapable that money that is allowed to remain fallow will gradually dwindle in real value, steadily losing its purchasing power.

What, then, can an individual do to protect the buying power of the surplus funds he sets aside for his future?

How is it possible to insulate money against the evaporative effects of prevailing—and reliably forecastable—inflationary economic winds?

The answer—are you with us, my dear Watson?—is elementary: Put the money to work, allowing—or, rather, compelling—it to earn its own keep and assure its own growth and future.

Money, odd as the concept may sound to more than a few people, possesses a remarkable willingness and capacity for performing remunerative work, and there are always limitless numbers and varieties of jobs open and waiting for it. But money, being a totally disenfranchised chattel, cannot select its own form of employment. Money must accept and perform whatever jobs its owner decides and directs it should take and do.

Now, when they first achieve any degree of fiscal elbow room and find they have funds surplus to their essential needs, most people put the money to work performing relatively simple and uncomplicated tasks. The employers to whom such people most commonly contract the services of their money are:

1. Banks.
2. Savings-and-loan associations.
3. Insurance companies.

These are wise, usually the wisest, ways in which beginners or individuals or families with comparatively slender financial resources can "hire out"—or, since it is time we start using the proper term, *invest*—their money.

Banks and savings-and-loan associations provide safe, secure and income-producing repositories for whatever funds a person wants to put aside as a "cash cushion."

Deposits with most institutions of both types are insured by the Federal Deposit Insurance Corporation or the Federal Savings and Loan Insurance Corporation. This means that the United States Government insures the depositor's money up to $15,000 for each individual account. (There are a few exceptions, and the tyro investor is well advised to proceed with caution before handing his money over to any institution in either category that is not covered by government insurance.)

Another characteristic shared by banks and S&LAs is that

they pay interest (sometimes called "dividends") on money deposited with them, often compounding the interest semi-annually or even quarterly—or sometimes daily. Withal, the safety and security provided by banks and S&LAs are "paid for" by two factors the investor should bear in mind and take into consideration:

1. The interest rates themselves are lower than the yields often offered by other, less safe and sure forms of investment.

2. Aside from interest payments—and, in the case of S&LAs, what are sometimes called "interest dividends"—there is no "growth" of the money deposited.

It should also be understood that banks and savings-and-loan associations are not at all the same thing. The differences in their organization, functions and operations are very great, but the major differences that are of interest to the average person can be explained briefly and easily.

When you open a savings account in a bank, you automatically become a creditor of the bank. For as long as you maintain your account, and whatever sums you deposit, the bank *owes* you the amount in the account, plus interest accrued and payable. If it is a "demand account"—the type most people are likely to have—you may withdraw all or any part of the money in it whenever you wish.

The bank must pay depositors immediately—"on demand."

There are, of course, other types of savings accounts, which are called "time-deposit accounts." In the case of such accounts, the depositor agrees to leave his money with the bank for a specified period of time—say, for a year. These accounts pay a slightly higher rate of interest than demand accounts. Nonetheless, under certain circumstances, depositors may withdraw their money before the agreed period is up, but there is an interest penalty. In any event, whatever type of savings account one has, the amounts on deposit are still debts owed to the depositor by the bank.

This is not true of savings-and-loan associations. An individual opening an account with an S&LA is not a creditor of the association. He is, in effect, buying a share of the association. The size of that share is the ratio of the amount in his account to the total of the amounts in all the association's accounts. For example, if Arthur Roe has $10,000 in an S&LA account and the sum of all accounts adds up to $2 million, then Roe's share is one two-thousandth.

Another significant difference between banks and savings-and-loan associations is that, at least in theory, the latter are not required to pay the account holder his money on demand. Laws and regulations governing the operations of savings-and-loan associations generally permit them to ask the account holder for a 30-day notice of intent to take out his money or any part of it. Furthermore, the money is not "withdrawn" in the same sense as it would be from a bank savings account. The S&LA account holder, being an owner and not a creditor, "sells back" his share—or such portion of his share as is represented by the amount he takes from his account—to the association.

(It is only fair to emphasize that, in practice, most well-managed savings-and-loan associations waive the 30-day-notice provision and "pay on demand." Also, it should be noted that the complex-sounding procedure of "selling back" one's share or portion thereof is merely a technicality, a legal formality that is usually taken care of in moments at the savings-and-loan association's counter.)

Most bank savings and savings-and-loan-association accounts serve as ideal means whereby the average individual can achieve three basic aims:

1. Common sense and ordinary prudence decree that everyone should have some sort and size of financial "cushion" in the form of readily available cash savings.

2. Whatever its dimensions, the "cushion" should be secure, sheltered from the sudden squalls that can cause sharp, more or less temporary, drops in the values of other investments—and it most certainly should be guaranteed against complete loss.

3. Money set aside to form a "financial cushion" should not be cached away in proverbial mattresses, in safety-deposit boxes or in places where it will lie dormant and unproductive.

It should be made to perform remunerative work and yield a return. That return may be allowed to accumulate and thereby increase the total of the money—of the principal—or it may be collected as income, spent or reinvested in other fields.

Altogether, cash savings that are deposited in insured, interest-paying accounts are the safest—and, for the tyro investor or person of limited means, the very best—of all investments. They provide a ready reserve against emergencies and contingencies. The interest the savings earn serves as a modest, but reassuring, hedge against inflation. The accounts themselves are the bases and nuclei upon and around which more elaborate investment structures may be built when larger sums of surplus cash become available.

It is for the individual to decide how he will distribute the funds he earmarks for savings. He has the three options of: putting all into bank savings accounts; putting all into savings-and-loan-association accounts; or splitting the money between the two. On the one hand, well-organized, efficiently run savings-and-loan associations tend to pay somewhat higher interest rates than banks. On the other, bank savings accounts are likely to carry with them certain "fringe benefits," such as easy access to the very wide range of special services that modern banks offer and perform for their clients.

Whatever your choice and decision, a note of warning: Although the great majority of United States banks and savings-and-loan associations are closely regulated, honest and reliable, there are still a few renegades around, preying on the unwary. For your own sake—and to be doubly certain you are not taking foolish and unnecessary risks with your hard-earned money—follow these simple rules before opening any form of savings account:

1. Ascertain whether or not the bank or S&LA in which you contemplate putting your money is insured by the Federal Deposit Insurance Corporation or the Federal Savings and Loan Insurance Corporation. If it isn't, find out why—and try to obtain a reliable, independent report on its reputation and financial condition.

2. If you have any other doubts—of any kind or for any reason—about a bank, savings-and-loan association or other financial institution, do not hesitate to ask questions. The nearest office of your Better Business Bureau is as good a place as any to begin your inquiries.

3. Above all, view with extreme suspicion and skepticism any banking firms, savings-and-loan associations or similar institutions that deluge you with advertisements promising astronomical interest rates on savings accounts or money deposited with them. This applies most particularly to such firms that are located outside the United States and thus not subject to the tight regulations and controls of American banking laws. Some of these foreign organizations are shaky; others are out-and-out swindles. Bear in mind that, in 1956–57, several hundred Tangier "banks" failed. Countless Americans who had been mesmerized by the pie-in-the-sky promises of 8.5 percent, 9 percent, 10 percent and even higher interest rates had transferred huge sums to these "banks," and when the collapse came, these gullible dupes lost untold millions of dollars.

In short, do not be afraid to shop the money market in the same way as you would any other market when seeking the best value for your dollars. And this advice applies with equal force to insurance, which is as popular a form of "basic" and "beginners" investment as are interest-paying savings accounts.

The array of different types, kinds, combinations and blends of life, endowment, annuity, retirement and kindred policies and insurance programs available today defies description. It would, methinks, require a volume thick with closely printed pages merely to list them—a project I am neither moved nor qualified to undertake. Suffice it to suggest—without much fear of being contradicted—that these days a good agent for a legitimate life insurance company is able to hand-tailor a policy or entire program to fit virtually any individual's situation and pocketbook.

Now, let me state my opinions regarding life insurance in the clearest and plainest possible terms.

I am in complete agreement with the principle that every person—and most particularly every person who has or expects or hopes to have a family—should have what, his individual situation and financial resources considered, is adequate life insurance coverage. And I agree with the life insurance salesmen's classic argument that "Life insurance is both investment and protection."

But—and it is a large *but*—I have observed that far too many people have a tendency to load themselves down with life insurance and annuity policies. The premiums on these policies eat up all the surplus funds they could put to work more profitably through other forms of investment. "Insurance poor" is a term familiar to all.

Insurance, sound and sensible as it is—and a must for any financial program—is nonetheless not the be all and end all of investment. As an *investment,* insurance offers a very small yield—unless, of course, the policyholder happens to drop dead far ahead of his time. The reason why the yield is small is completely understandable: a goodly portion of the investment pays for the protection a life policy offers, thereby absorbing much of what would otherwise be the return.

As for annuity policies, either pencil, paper and computations—or any frank and honest insurance man—will reveal that about all they actually offer is a systematic return of the policyholders' money, on such dates and in such amounts as are set forth in the insurance-policy contract.

There should be a sane and reasonable approach to insurance if the individual is not to saddle himself with a hodge-podge of policies and a back-breaking burden of premium payments. Most impartial observers agree that the following set of guidelines are helpful to any person who is desirous of having good insurance protection without overstraining his budget and preventing himself from making other and more lucrative investments:

1. At the beginning, when your income is limited, obtain the necessary amount of life insurance—but buy convertible and renewable term policies. You get more face value per dollar—and later, when you are earning more money, you can begin converting the policies gradually.

2. Insurance of any kind should only be purchased from well-established, highly reputable companies through agents or brokers of equal caliber. Some states have rather loose laws governing the operations of insurance companies—and insurance is a field that has its share of fly-by-nights and gyps. Always check on both the company and the agent or broker; once more, you can initiate your inquiries at your local Better Business Bureau. That admirable watchdog agency will give you additional leads if it is unable to supply all the necessary information.

3. Never—but never—purchase any insurance without first obtaining a specimen copy of the policy you intend buying. Study it carefully, reading all the fine-print clauses. If you do not or cannot understand them—and after the fifth *whereas,* sixth *hereinabove* and a few triple negatives, anyone is liable to get lost—take the document to your attorney or some other completely reliable and qualified person for translation.

4. What the salesman promises or implies means nothing —unless all he says is stated in writing in the policy. If there is any appreciable difference between the sales talk and the printed word, this should serve as an alarm signal.

5. Make certain that your policy is delivered to you soon after you have "bought" it. Be suspicious of any broker or agent who stalls or delays delivery of a policy.

6. Shop for values in buying insurance—but don't under any circumstances buy bargains, because there are none. Policies that are peddled at prices considerably below those set for like policies by old-line companies are often studded with so many escape clauses as to be next to worthless. (On the other hand, some excellent insurance "buys" are available through cooperatives and from certain smaller companies that are in excellent financial condition, but can offer reduced premiums because they pare their administrative and other overhead expenses to the bone. Such companies will receive top recommendations from Better Business Bureaus and similar agencies, and are thus readily identifiable from the gyps.)

By starting a savings account and purchasing the insurance he needs and can afford, the average individual makes two astute investments. He can feel that he has taken two long strides toward assuring his financial future.

And, as he watches his savings grow, the value of his insurance policies increase and receives increases in salary, he begins to champ at the bit. He feels himself ready to graduate—to try his hand at more sophisticated forms of investment.

Whereupon, he takes the next stride. . . .

16 NEXT RUNGS ON THE INVESTMENT LADDER

Having accumulated some savings—the "cash cushion"— and purchased a reasonable amount of insurance, the average person "graduates" into investing in United States Savings Bonds. After that, he will most probably invest in common stocks. Some advice —and more than a few warnings— about investing money in stocks. While there are no hard-and-fast rules which guarantee successful investment in common shares, there are guides and safeguards that help the average investor reduce risks and increase his chances for successful investment.

As a rule, after having established a savings account and purchased insurance, the next stage in the average person's investment career involves buying United States Savings Bonds, which, as investments, are unique unto themselves.

Why are they so different? The reasons are best explained in a roundabout manner:

1. As it is understood and applies in the business world, a bond is definable as a formal evidence of a debt, whereby the borrower promises to pay the lender a specified amount with interest at a fixed rate payable on specified dates. Fur-

thermore, the indebtedness represented by the bond is generally secured by a definite mortgage on property owned by
the borrower. (This is why businessmen frequently speak of
senior industrial bonds being "first mortgages on the assets
of the company.")

2. Now a *debenture* bond is—again according to business
definition—very similar to an ordinary bond in all respects
save that it is not secured by a mortgage on property, but
rather it is backed by the general credit and overall assets of
the borrower.

Obviously, the United States Government cannot very well
mortgage any of its property—which belongs to the American people, to the public. Thus, in the event the United
States Treasury defaulted on payment of bonds issued by it,
the bondholders could not go into court and seek a writ of
seizure against a battleship, a post-office building or a national park to satisfy the debt.

By a similar token, the United States Government possesses
assets in only the very broadest sense—for those assets derive
from, belong and revert to the public, the nation as a whole.
Or, to put it another way, American citizens purchasing
United States Government bonds are loaning money to themselves against property and assets owned by themselves. And
they will be paying themselves interest and repaying their
own loans.

Yet, while United States Savings Bonds do not yield spectacular rates of interest—and, of course, offer no possibilities
for "growth"—they are indubitably the safest of any securities in which an individual may invest his money.

"Government bonds can break only if the government itself breaks," is an observation one often hears voiced. "And
if that ever happens, it will mean that everything else has already crumbled into nothing."

An overstatement? No, not really. It is just a dramatic—
if oblique—way of underlining that the collateral securing
government bonds consists of the integrity of the nation and
the strength and vitality of its political and economic systems.

Almost without exception, the type of United States Government bond that the neophyte investor will buy is the

Series "E" Savings Bond. These bonds are issued in denominations (denoting value at maturity) ranging upward from $10. Series "E" bonds are nontransferable and nonmarketable; they cannot be sold or otherwise transferred to any person other than the original purchaser (although they may be "co-owned," as by husband and wife), and their value is fixed, not subject to market fluctuation. They must be held for a minimum period of sixty days after purchase, but may be "cashed in" for their full accrued value at any time thereafter.

Many people at all income levels make a regular practice of buying a Series "E" Savings Bond of a certain denomination at set intervals—for example, a $50 bond each month. Those who do so declare they derive a very warm and comforting sense of security from watching their "collection" of bonds grow larger—and their value increase—over the years.

There are several other types of United States Savings and Treasury bonds, among them issues that are transferable and marketable. The denominations of some Treasury bonds go from $50 to one million dollars. However, by the time an individual begins to buy United States Government bonds of other than the Series "E" Savings type, it is very likely that he has become a comparatively sophisticated investor—that he has already branched out in other directions, diversifying his investments.

There is widespread agreement among financial authorities that, insofar as investment in securities is concerned, after they have accumulated some Series "E"s most people are inclined to take the big leap and start investing in common stocks. This contention would appear to be borne out by the fact that there are somewhere in the neighborhood of twenty million individual common stockholders in the United States today. Financial advisers, brokers and others who deal regularly with the stock-buying public claim the average individual is motivated to invest in common shares by a process of reasoning that goes somewhat as follows:

1. I have accumulated a "cash cushion" of savings—but my savings account pays only modest interest, and the value of my capital thus invested cannot apreciate beyond whatever amounts it may earn in the form of interest.

2. I also have what I consider to be adequate life insurance. This provides protection for the members of my family in the event anything happens to me. However, I am deriving no present income from the money I have put to work paying the premiums, and even with the most liberal annuity policies, the benefits I will receive are much deferred.

3. My United States Government Savings Bonds are providing additional supersafe security, both for the present and for the future. But they, too, have a low annual yield. Therefore, they will not "grow" very much or very rapidly, either.

4. Considering that I have these solid bulwarks to shield me—and my family—from financial disaster, I am now in a position to take some risks with my surplus funds with a view to making them earn greater returns and rewards.

5. The most logical answer is to begin investing in common stocks, which offer the double-barreled potential of immediate income and increase in capital through "growth" in their value.

The decision to buy common stocks can be a most wise and profitable one for any person who desires to augment his income, increase his capital and guarantee the security—even the comfort—of his and his family's future. It can also be a move that will produce only indifferent results, yielding no more return than if the funds involved had been deposited into an interest-paying savings account or used to purchase Savings Bonds. Or, it can—and not infrequently does—prove to be a very bad decision leading to painful losses or even fiscal debacle.

Believe me—and I speak as one who has bought millions of shares of stock during my career—the decision to put money to work in the stock market is not a decision to be taken lightly. Money used to buy stocks—be they common or preferred, purchased in single-share lots or 100,000-share blocks—is money that is being risked.

There are *no* surefire get-rich-quick schemes or formulas on "Wall Street." If there were, every stockbroker, financial adviser and investment counselor would have gone out of business long ago—to wallow in Oriental splendors and luxuries on their accumulated millions and tens of millions. Yet, anyone—even the greenest novice—has the capacity to reduce the risks involved to an absolute minimum and to increase his chances for achieving desired aims and objectives to an absolute maximum.

How?

Very simply and easily. The tried and proved modus operandi calls for adhering to the same clear-cut basic rules and principles that are—and always will be—the operative "secrets" of all successful investors. Ask anyone who has consistently made profits in the stock market, and he will tell you that:

1. The most important key is to be found in the word "invest."

Sound, carefully selected common stocks are potentially excellent *investments*—and they should be purchased as and for investments and *not* for purposes of speculation. Far more often than not, the individual who "goes out to make a big, quick killing" does precisely that and on a grand scale—by annihilating his capital.

Despite all the advances that have been made in the science of meteorology, it is still folly to bet ahead on the weather. The sun may shine brightly today—but there is no way of telling for certain that there will not be a thunder shower within the coming week or ten days. On the other hand, the *climate* follows fairly regular and predictable patterns. One does not take any very great hazards by wagering that, ten years hence, the summers will be warmer than the winters.

The stock market speculator is spiritual blood brother to the compulsive, reckless plunger—a "cowboy" in the argot of professional gamblers—who would bet, and give long odds to boot, that there won't be a cloud visible anywhere in the sky at 11:35 A.M. a week from next Thursday. He is, in short, an emotional, irrational gambler who commits too much of his resources on too slender a possibility at the wrong odds. And, like all such gamblers, although he may win once or twice, it is certain that he will "play back" all his winnings and end up losing his original stake as well. Neither his temperament nor his methods equip him to think objectively, play coolly or cope with temporary setbacks.

The investor, by contrast, takes a long, hard and analytical look at the historical patterns of the climate. When he is fully conversant with these—and is able to obtain the most favorable odds—he banks his money on the probability that there will be no radical changes of long duration in the established patterns. He "plays" the stock market cerebrally, not emotionally, purchasing stocks with long-range intent and purpose.

Any investor worthy of the name—and deserving of the rewards he is very likely to reap—knows that the long-term trend of the economy and all its component elements is a rising trend. Thus, with patient assurance, he waits for the stock dividends and the steady increases in per-share values that will, over a period of years or decades, multiply his investment. Dips, drops, recessions and even depressions do not cause him to panic; they do not even ruffle his calm, for he has made the requisite allowances and preparations for such eventualities. The unmistakable mark of the successful investor is that he realizes there are infinitely greater profits to be earned by holding on to a good stock than through any number of overnight coups.

It is a desire to emphasize this basic home truth and not any impulse to boast or gloat that moves me to mention that I—and innumerable other seasoned investors—today own issues worth one hundred or even more times what we originally paid for them. And this leads us directly to another open secret of stock market success.

2. The astute investor not only understands that he must give his stocks time to increase in value, but he also possesses a good sense of timing.

Before me as I write these words is a graph charting the course of the Dow-Jones Industrial Averages since 1913. The present level is more than twenty times higher than it was in 1913. It is self-evident that the overall trend to which I have previously referred has been *up* for more than half a century. However—and this is the crux—within that clear, unequivocal *long-term* trend there are many cycles, or, if you prefer, many rises and falls.

The rises indicate what stock market professionals call "bull markets," periods when more people were inclined to buy than to sell, and hence the prices of shares were bid higher. The falls—"bear markets"—are indicative of exactly the opposite; for whatever reasons, the pressure was to sell, rather than to buy, and stock prices consequently drifted (or, as in 1929, plummeted) down.

The graph line shows that every drop was eventually followed by a rebound that carried the Dow-Jones Averages to a peak higher than the previous top level. And, after each new peak was reached, there has always been another decline. In other words, the line is a series of sharp upward zigs and downward zags, with the zigs reaching progressively higher peaks.

It is in this context that the investor's sense of timing serves as a paramount factor in determining whether or not he will be successful in the stock market. The "secret" is knowing *when* to buy.

Now, only a very foolish person would be willing to pay $100 today to purchase an item for which he did not have an absolute, immediate need if he knew the same item was to be placed on sale tomorrow at $75. By the same token, the shrewd investor with a well-developed sense of timing buys stocks when their prices have been driven down by temporary "bear market" cycles and not when they are at or near their "bull market" peaks.

No, of course not. The investor cannot know for certain that Windfall and Fortune common will be "marked down" and "placed on sale" at a bargain price on this, that or another day. But he can, on the basis of historical precedent, safely assume that every upward spiral or surge of prices will reach a peak—and that the peak will be followed by a downward adjustment before a new "bull" cycle develops.

I have said that the investor—as opposed to the speculator—is patient and able to wait for his investments to increase in value. The same quality of patience enables him to wait calmly until the time is ripe for making purchases. He is not a compulsive buyer who allows himself to be carried along by stampeding herds of bulls; nor will he follow the crowd of speculators and unsophisticated hopefuls who are bidding prices up and up. Instead, he watches from the sidelines. When the speculators and herd-instinct buyers have been shaken out and prices have once more readjusted to realistic levels, he buys.

But the investor most likely to succeed in the stock market does not buy blindly or haphazardly, nor does he pay heed to tips or hunches. He refuses to get his fingers burned by grabbing at "hot tips," "hot issues" or stocks overheated by fevered speculators. Instead . . .

3. The shrewd investor subjects any stock to a rigorous prepurchase examination and, before investing a penny, insists it meet at least these minimum requirements:

● The Federal Securities and Exchange Commission keeps a keenly alert regulatory eye on the activities of public-stock companies. Unfortunately, it cannot always and at the same time see into every dark nook and cranny of the business world. Consequently, as a general rule, the experienced investor obtains an extra margin of safety by purchasing only such stocks as are listed on major stock exchanges. Fear of loss through fraud or misrepresentation is by no means the only reason for hewing to this rule. Even when an unlisted stock and the company issuing it are completely honest and reliable— and most are—the investor who buys unlisted shares may find himself "locked in," because it isn't always easy to find ready buyers for unlisted shares. Nor is it always possible to establish their fair market values; since they are not traded on an exchange, the laws of supply and demand which establish the price levels of listed securities are not operative.

● Even when a stock is listed on a major exchange—and even the "Big Board" itself—the wise investor digs deep to obtain all the information available that may have any bearing or influence on the prospects and potentials of the stock and the company issuing it.

- The first item on the agenda is a survey of the field or industry in which the company is operating. It must be one with a future. It is ridiculous to invest money in a field or industry producing goods or performing services which may become obsolescent or obsolete within a few years.

- Assuming that the outlook is satisfactory, the next question is how the company stands in relation to its competitors. Needless to say, it should be doing more than merely holding its own.

- The company's past performance is a matter of vital interest. Much revealing data may be obtained by studying its annual reports—and the financial statements contained therein—for a period going back several years. In their sum, the reports should reflect progress (however, a bad year or two does not necessarily mean there is anything wrong; all companies have their occasional slump spells).

- The overall picture of the corporation's earnings, profits and dividends records must emerge sound and satisfactory. The price of its stock ought to show a reasonable degree of growth over the years. Patterns reflecting unwarranted, erratic price convulsions provide grounds for deep suspicion.

- In the final analysis, whatever its size or nature, a business organization is made up of people—and those people can make or break the organization. Constant changes, shifting and shufflings of top-level managerial personnel and a long history of labor strife do not augur well for the future of any company. Conversely, reasonably stable management, good employee morale and a low labor turnover rate are strong plus factors and excellent recommendations; they mean the organization is functioning as a team to achieve desired results.

Yes, I'll admit that much dogged research, intensive study and hard work would be—and are—needed to gather all the information outlined above. But then, sound investment in common stocks calls for more than just snap decisions and

money—far more, if the investor is to have a better than me-
diocre chance of being successful and earning good profits
from his investments.

In order to view the entire subject in proper perspective
and a clear, revealing light, try projecting yourself into the
following imaginary situation:

Suppose you have $20,000 in surplus capital, want to go
into business for yourself and are in the market to buy a
drugstore, service station, haberdashery or any other type of
established business enterprise for which you may have a
preference.

Are you "in the picture"? Fine, then imagine that one afternoon you receive a telephone call from Walter Blake, a casual
acquaintance.

"I've heard of just the business you're looking to buy!" he
announces enthustically. He proceeds to tell you in the
vaguest—but superlative-studded—terms about a store or
shop or whatever that is located halfway across the continent,
in a city you've never seen.

"You'd better buy it, right away!" Blake urges. "The price
is $20,000, and I know a person right here in town who can
close the deal for you within an hour!"

What would be your reaction?

Would you buy the business, sight unseen, without exam-
ining the establishment, looking over the current owner's
books and otherwise doing your utmost to determine if it is
a going concern with good prospects and potentials?

I doubt very seriously that you would. In fact, I am certain that you would not.

Why then should you—or anyone else—buy a part of a
business (which is precisely what you do when you invest in
common stocks) without taking equal care and precautions?

Yet, every working day of the year, countless otherwise
sane and sensible people are investing their hard-earned capital on recommendations and "tips" no more solid and reliable than "Walter Blake's" telephone patter. They are buying
into companies about which they know little or nothing—
save, perhaps, that "someone said it was a good thing."

If the point isn't crystal clear, try thinking of it this way:
When you purchase a corporation's stocks, you are not

only buying a piece of the corporation, you are also sending your capital off, a long way from home, to work for you *in* the company. If you have any regard at all for that capital, you will want to know under what sort of conditions it will be working and have some idea of the "salary" it will earn and what opportunities the company offers it for advancement and growth. Your capital deserves tender care and solicitude —and the effort required to select the most enlightened and progressive organizations as its employers.

Like it or not, you must face the fact that there are always elements of risk present when you invest in the stock market. The hazards and imponderables can never be eliminated completely. But it is possible to reduce their numbers and greatly decrease the menace of those that remain.

As has been remarked, the process of preshrinking the perils and thereby expanding the chances for profits requires patience, a sense of timing and much hard work. Successful investors gladly take all the time, trouble and effort necessary to bring the risks down to irreducible minimums.

That is why they are successful.

And that is why they retire with ostrich-size nest eggs and comfortable incomes instead of melancholy memories of missed opportunities and financial fiascos.

17 AS THE INVESTOR BECOMES MORE SOPHISTICATED

Some observations regarding mutual funds—and then a close look at real estate. Common-sense guides and rules for home buying. Trading up. The opportunities—and the risks—of investing in real estate. Suggestions for gaining the greatest profit from real estate— and notes on how to avoid unnecessary losses. Ideas for the retired person who finds that his home is too large for his needs now that his children are married. Four possible options and possibilities —and four advantages to certain types of real estate investment.

The reader is very probably wondering why no reference was made in the previous chapter to mutual funds, the highly popular means whereby the individual with limited financial resources may diversify, broaden the base of his investment in securities. The omission was purely intentional, and for these reasons:

1. There are some hundreds of these mutual funds—"open-end" investment companies—in operation at the present time, and more new ones are being organized each year. All share a common trait, or principle, of operation. Mutual funds invest in the securities of various companies (and, in some instances and to greater or lesser degrees, also in such securities as municipal bonds). Mutual funds obtain the money to invest by selling their own shares to the public. But, from this point, the similarities begin to grow less distinct—and, in fact, there are many very different types of mutual funds, among them:

- Those which invest only in common stocks.
- Mutual funds which invest in common *and* preferred stocks.
- Investment companies of the "open-end" variety that seek to achieve "balance" by purchasing a broad range of securities.
- "Flexible" mutual funds whose policy it is to switch emphasis and the proportions of amounts invested as the current situation or indicated trends suggest would be more advantageous or as, if and when their managements deem such shifts advisable.
- Mutual funds which "narrow down" or "focus" by limiting their investments to securities in certain industries.
- Mutual funds which invest exclusively in the shares of other mutual funds.

2. As perhaps may be guessed from the foregoing, the aims and objectives of various mutual funds also differ greatly, as *vide infra* the partial listing of typical examples:

- Some seek primarily to provide their shareholders with steady income.
- Others make "growth"—the increase of per-share value —their paramount goal.
- Yet others aim for "conservation of capital," the maintenance of capital at a constant value level.
- Then, of course, there are those mutual funds which operate with a view toward achieving the best of all possible worlds by combining all these objectives into one package.

3. With such broad spectrums of possibilities and combinations of possibilities present, any discussion of mutual funds would necessarily wend a tortuous path along labyrinthine detours and byways. No practical conclusions of value to all—or even a majority—could be reached. No definitive overall guidelines could be established, for in all instances, the final and determining factors lie with and within the individual investor himself.

4. In any event, as this book is being written, there are many reports current regarding recommendations and projected moves to effect certain changes in the operations of open-end investment companies. Whether or not any actual changes will be made is a moot question at this time. Many months will undoubtedly elapse before final decisions are reached and the situation is clarified. Thus, any more detailed remarks or observations regarding mutual funds that could be made here would have to be based on presently existing practices and procedures. These could, perforce, prove to be inaccurate and misleading by the time the book is published.

5. Nevertheless, now—or in the future—the basic rules and principles of sound investment in common stock can be said to apply with equal validity and vigor, and with only slight modifications, to investment in mutual funds. The wise investor will conduct meticulous preliminary investigations and make painstaking comparisons of the various funds and their plans, programs and portfolios before buying shares in any of them. He will seek to determine which have the best record of performance, are most closely tailored to meet the specifications of his own situation, needs and aims—present and future—and offer him the best prospects and most promise for successful investment.

I hasten to reiterate that my remarks concerning mutual funds have been distilled down to a comparatively brief précis for the reasons I have cited—and for no others. Lest there be any possibility of misunderstanding, I wish to make it abundantly clear that no doubts or criticisms of open-end investment companies are intended or implied. Widely published reports offer ample evidence that most mutual funds have performed well over the years, and that more than a few have netted very large profits for their shareholders. If—and I repeat the if loudly and clearly—there are any wolves among the sheep, they are no more numerous than in any other fold, and the astute investor, always aware of the principle of *caveat emptor,* knows how to spot the rough pelts among the soft and golden fleece.

That said, we can turn and devote our attention and the remainder of this chapter to one of the oldest forms of "investment" known to man, namely what is today called "real estate" or "real property"—land, the improvements on it and its natural assets/resources.

The desire of human beings to possess land of their own can be traced back so far in history that one might be moved to surmise it is little short of an innate instinctual drive. And the concepts of land and the improvements on it as property that can be owned, to which an individual may have title, and which he can transfer are almost as ancient. "Documents" in the form of cuneiform tablets that are concerned with establishing or transferring title to land and buildings are among some of the earliest written records that have come down to us through the ages.

Furthermore, the ownership of land has traditionally placed a man above and apart from those of his fellows who owned no "real property." In the armies of Hammurabi, the most menial tasks were automatically assigned to those who did not own land. In much later eras, the term "propertied classes" usually referred to those persons who held title to real property and implied—in the main, correctly—that such ownership endowed them with special rights, privileges and powers not shared by the "landless."

These sharp distinctions separating the "propertied" minority from the "landless" and thus greatly disadvantaged majority have been gradually blurring and disappearing. Nevertheless, the urge to own land and structures built uppon it still remains strong—and the opportunity for doing so is open to almost all.

Nowadays, tens of millions of Americans own or are buying real estate—mainly in the form of homes. Oddly enough, while aware that they are acquiring real property, many homeowners do not seem to consider or understand themselves to be investors—and long-term investors at that. Real estate men—or, by preferred, glossier appellation, realtors—report frequent encounters with clients who are unable to conceive of the purchase of the proverbial vine-covered cottages or stylish split-level mortgage manors as investments.

"But we're actually going to *live* in the house, use it ourselves," such individuals are wont to protest. "How on earth can the roof over our heads be considered an investment? Why, it's preposterous!"

The difficulty, realtors conclude, stems from a muddled concept of what constitutes investment in real estate or a real estate investment. Some people evidently think that only properties bought specifically to produce income (from rents, farming, etc.) or to make a profit (by resale at higher prices in a rising market or after subdivision or improvement) qualify as investments.

Such ideas are, needless to say, wholly erroneous. That the owner and his family live in the house and romp in the garden does not in any fashion alter the fact that their property is an investment—that the money it cost them was invested in the property. Of course, the investment may be good, bad or indifferent, for like any other form of investment, real estate possesses a potential for increasing in value, but it also carries with it a certain amount of risk. The value of any real property—including a house and lot—may, over the years, or in some cases virtually overnight, increase or decrease, or it may remain at approximately the same level as it was at the time of purchase.

The key characteristic of real estate is implicit in the qualifying adjective; it is "real" in the sense that it is tangible, fixed, enduring a hereditament. A piece of land, be it 50 by 125-foot residential plot or 10,000-acre tract, remains land that can be owned, used for various purposes, handed down from one generation to the next. Provided it is well built, properly maintained and no calamities such as fire or flood destroy or damage it beyond repair, a house or other structure will "last" and continue to serve useful purposes for scores or even hundreds of years.

All other things being equal, an individual buying real estate is not acquiring an item of property that will wear out in a short time or even during his lifetime. If for no other reason than this, the purchase of real estate is a true long-term investment, an exchange of money—or of capital, if you prefer—for something that has an inherent quality of durability, even of permanence.

A person who purchases a house and lot (or, for that matter, a cooperative apartment), or buys a plot of ground and then builds a house on it to live in, should most definitely realize from the very beginning that he *is* making an investment. The property will not only serve as a home; it will be a fixed asset with an ascertainable, realizable money value.

However, I feel compelled to reiterate that, real as real estate is, and though it frequently offers fine opportunities for "growth" of the capital that has been invested in it, real estate can also be a risky form of investment. Yes, there are countless stories—mostly true—about individuals who bought homes for, say, $5,000 just before World War II began, lived in them for 20 or 25 years and then sold the properties for three, four or even more times their original purchase price. Conversely, and notwithstanding the upward spiral of real property values, there are equally true tales of people who suffered heavy losses.

"This year's swamp may be next year's suburban development" is an old adage among realtors. "And today's mansion may be tomorrow's tenement."

To which might be added that it is also entirely possible that the swamp will remain a swamp—and the mansion will remain a mansion.

Since, for most families, real estate investment will be largely—or often entirely—limited to home purchasing, let us peruse this area more closely. Home-buying patterns are usually decided by two variable influences which, though separate and distinct from each other, are very likely to operate concurrently.

The first of these factors is economic. At the beginning of his career, a husband and father usually has a relatively low income. As a consequence, he is strictly limited in the amount he can pay—or which he can obligate himself—for the purchase of a home. He buys a small, simple house and then, as his income rises, he "trades up," acquiring successively larger and more elaborate homes.

The second factor is the amount of living space required—or, stated another way, the size of the family that will occupy the home. As a rule, families buying their first house consist of husband and wife and, perhaps, one child. Their requirements for living space are therefore satisfied by a few rooms. Later, if there are more children, the original house becomes cramped, too small to meet the family's needs for adequate living space. Again, the pressure is to "trade up" by purchasing a larger house.

(Some farsighted individuals make advance allowance for this second factor when buying their first house. They make certain there is ample additional land and the house possesses the necessary features to permit expansion by building on extra rooms as and when needed.)

Both these pressures tend to create a long-term pattern that may be likened to an inverted *V*. As the years pass, increasing income and growing family continue to motivate the "trading up" process until a peak is reached. Thereafter, the likelihood is that the need for living space will decrease as children marry and move away from home, and the husband-father's earnings, too, have peaked. With retirement, they drop or slope down to some extent or another.

At this juncture, the homeowner is faced with a dilemma —what to do with a house that has become far too big for his wife and himself?

Before considering the many optional answers to that question, let us retrace our steps all the way back to the starting line and build a pyramid of common-sense rules for sound real estate investment on the skeleton provided by the inverted *V* outline that has already been drawn.

The fundamental principles of sound real estate investment are very similar to those applying to almost any other form of investment:

1. Obtain the best possible value for your money.
2. Buy as an investor, not as a speculator.
3. Reduce your risks of loss.
4. Do all you can to increase your chances for increasing the value of the capital you invest.

There are several major practical rules that should be followed by all home-buying real estate investors including:

1. Determine how much you can afford to spend for a home—either in cash or in cash-plus-mortgage obligation—without overextending yourself. Bear in mind that ownership of a house involves many costs and expenses that do not increase your equity in the property or necessarily add a penny to its value; among them are:

- Interest on the mortgage (if any).
- Property taxes and assessments.
- Insurance.
- Maintenance of house and grounds.
- Heating and utilities.
- If buying the house means moving from city to suburbs as it so often does these days—commutation costs must also be taken into consideration.

2. The magic formula for shrewd financing of home investment is to pay cash—all cash and at one time. In the first place, this eliminates all mortgage interest; in the second, anyone able to pay all cash is almost certain to receive a price concession or discount. However, very few people have enough surplus capital to buy their homes for cash. For them, the slightly less magical—but still extremely effective—formula is to make as large a down payment as possible and obtain a mortgage that covers the balance at the lowest possible interest rate. Incidentally, the particularly astute home-buying investor will seek to obtain a mortgage that gives him the privilege of paying it off prior to expiration date with little or no penalty. Don't be afraid to shop around for the best mortgage "bargains."

3. Deal only through reputable, licensed real estate brokers.

4. Examine any and all papers, contracts, agreements or other documents you may be required to sign under the strongest microscope. Better still, have an attorney you can trust with complete confidence comb through every paragraph and line.

5. Always buy title insurance on any property you purchase. The cost is minimal—and it can save you enormous amounts of time, trouble *and* money.

So much for some of the more important financial points. Now, what about picking the house itself? The main rule here is to move with infinite care and caution; no matter what the glib salesman for the builders of Actfast Acres says, it is *not* imperative that you buy right now, today. Beyond that, never fail to:

1. Make certain the house you intend buying is suited to your family, its requirements, its own group characteristics (each family has its own)—and to you.

2. Are you an expert on building construction? If you are, then you can examine the house yourself. If you are not, have the job done for you by someone who is an expert and can judge if the structure is well put together and free of potentially costly flaws.

3. Obtain an independent appraisal of the value of the house.

4. Check the neighborhood. It should be old enough to have assumed some character and flavor—and if these are not as you want them, move on to happier house-hunting grounds.

5. Investigate—with great thoroughness—the zoning laws that apply to the neighborhood or area.

6. Last—as first and foremost—remember that you are not in the market for a $2.98 item that will wear out within six months' time. You are on the verge of *investing* thousands— or tens of thousands—of dollars in real property.

Now, let us assume that you have followed all the rules throughout the years and have successfully progressed from small, mass-produced bungalow through three-bedroom ranch-style to seven- or eight-room colonial-style. You are now past 50, the last of your children has just gotten married, you and your wife are rattling around in a house much too large for your actual requirements and, within a few years, you will be retiring.

What now?

First—and I've made mention of this elsewhere—be sure that, no matter what you may decide, the mortgage on the house can be paid off by the time you retire. I say "can" rather than "will" be paid off because, as yet, you do not know what you want to do with the house. You have a large number of options:

1. For sentimental—or other—reasons, you may want to keep the house and continue living in it. In that case, be certain that your postretirement income will be ample to cover all household costs, including maintenance, repairs and, naturally, taxes.

2. You want to retain ownership of the house, but you do not want to continue living in it. You want a much smaller place. Fine. See about the possibilities of leasing or renting the "big" house. The rental income may be sufficient to cover all your owner's costs and expenses and leave you a tidy margin of clear income besides.

3. The house is worth much more than you originally paid for it. Now is a good time to sell. The amount you realize may be sufficient to buy a fine small house in Florida, California, Arizona—provided you want to move to those or any other states after retirement—and leave you enough to cover the rent of a small house or apartment in your own city until "R Day" arrives. Also, the "retirement house" you buy in the warmer, more relaxing locales traditionally preferred by retired persons may produce income through rent until you are ready to move into it.

4. Is there a housing shortage in your area? Unless there are zoning laws preventing it, why not give consideration to converting your large one-family house into two or more apartments? You and your wife can live in one while you rent the other—or others. Or you can leave the resulting duplex, triplex or whatever in the hands of a reliable agent and go wherever you wish—with the rental income coming in regularly each month.

These are only a few of the many possibilities—and all are sound, practical and potentially profitable.

But persons nearing or reaching retirement very often find

that they have much to gain through other forms of real estate investment, especially if they want to keep busy and augment their incomes after they retire. Many who are especially perspicacious and provident begin investing early in apartment houses, resort hotels, motels or similar properties which offer an ideal combination of attractions and advantages:

1. They are fixed, durable capital assets.
2. Such properties produce income.
3. They provide living quarters as well as income for their owner. The retired person can thus have his home right on his business premises without sacrificing any of the accustomed amenities—and, in fact, enjoying several special benefits.
4. Last—but very far from least—active management of the property, of the "business," cannot help but keep the retired individual productive and young in heart and spirit.

One man I know of improvised what—at least for him—was a clever and imaginative variation on this basic theme. When he reached 53, he bought some beach property on New York's Fire Island. Over the next seven years, he built a total of eight small, simple summer cottages on the property. He had them constructed one at a time, as and when he had enough surplus cash to pay all the building costs. His wife did her part by shopping carefully to obtain the necessary minimal furnishings at low prices. Upon retirement, this man owned eight cottages, each of which produces a summer-season rental income of upward of $1,000.

"I 'work' four months each year, living in one of the cottages and keeping my eye on the others," he declares happily. "My maintenance and all other business costs and expenses total about $2,000 a year—the rest is profit. When the summer season is over and the weather turns chilly, my wife and I head south, to Florida. You see, we own a duplex down there. The half we rent out carries the building—and even pays for operating and maintaining our 36-foot cabin cruiser. . . ."

It should be added that this individual was not a businessman or an executive during his active career. He was a skilled

mechanic who worked his way up to be an assistant produc
tion-line foreman.

Little wonder that so many people swear by real estat
and claim that, if care and caution are exercised, it can b
one of the soundest, most rewarding forms of investment.

18 THE ALCHEMY THAT TURNS RETIREMENT INTO A GOLDEN AGE

The "senior citizen" of today has a very wide choice of opportunities open to him when he retires. He has many potentially productive years ahead of him after he leaves his job. It is for the individual to decide how he wants to spend those years—and, if he chooses wisely, he will find that a new and extremely gratifying life lies ahead of him. He will be entering into a Golden Age, a fully qualified connoisseur of the art of living.

When young men are thrown together in the same environment for any long period—as in college or the military services—they frequently form into groups for the purpose of continuing their association and establishing business enterprises after graduation or discharge.

On the face of things, they have much in their favor: youth, ambition, enthusiasm, energy and an already proved abilit to coexist and interact with each other. Unfortunately, v few of the enterprises thus formed ever succeed. The majority fail—sometimes due to lack of adequate capi much more often because the young men do not po necessary experience and seasoning. They may have ample theoretical knowledge—but have not been through the hard mill that teaches how to handle situations that are not covered by the book.

What never ceases to amaze me is why men who are at the other end of the chronological age scale, know each other well and work together in harmony do not more often form similar groups for similar purposes after they "graduate" from their regular jobs into that new stage of life known as retirement. Admittedly, a man of 60 or 65 does not have the burning fervors of a 20- or 25-year-old youth. But he should still have ambition, a goodly supply of energy and enthusiasm. And he possesses—by virtue of having earned them the hard way—two priceless additional assets: experience and time.

It would seem to me that three, four or more men who have spent many years learning and doing various types of work in a given field could combine their knowledge and experience and offer invaluable services as advisers and consultants to commercial and industrial firms. Many men have already done just this after retirement—and have achieved remarkable success. The big question in my mind is why haven't more followed suit?

Certainly, the seasoned middle-aged individual who has encountered a myriad of problems—and solved them—during his active career can very frequently come up with instant solutions to dilemmas that defy resolution by the best of younger, less experienced heads and hands. This is particularly true because the retired individual is able to concentrate his mind and efforts on the immediate matter; since his time is entirely his own, he is not distracted by other problems and issues.

now that I, for one—and I am hardly alone among busi-
would be very glad to have the standby services of
ialists available to help younger executives
lems that stump them and slow down
hich they have control.
ssential that retired men organize or asso-
ve advice and counsel or perform practical
dual who knew his job well can keep right
ive work and offering valuable services after

of exchange with which the retired person is most liberally supplied: experience, seasoned common sense and time.

On display and there for the "buying" are civic projects and problems; community affairs; local, state and national political matters; church, service club and charity activities and a dazzling array of other "things to do."

There are "items" to suit every taste at "prices" within every range of personal capacity and desire for involvement.

A traffic light is badly needed at the intersection of Third and Elm streets; someone is needed to organize the residents of the neighborhood and bring the necessary pressure to bear on the appropriate city bureaus and officials.

There aren't enough crossing guards to protect the children attending the local elementary school.

The city hospital is an antiquated eyesore, inside and out.

Five thousand more signatures are needed on a petition to halt a needless pork-barrel project that will cost the citizens millions.

A hundred thousand dollars needs to be collected—by door-to-door solicitation—for the Community Chest.

The Salvation Army is asking for volunteers with special skills to help as teachers in an occupational therapy program.

A centennial celebration is being planned.

John H. Doe, the best-qualified and most deserving candidate for Mayor or Congressman or Governor or President, needs all the help he can get in his campaign.

The city is dragging its feet on civil rights and antipoverty programs.

Volunteers are needed to form a working committee to improve racial relations in the community.

People are being asked to visit and spend time with crippled ex-servicemen at the nearby veterans' hospital.

The Rotary Club is about to hold its annual picnic for orphan children. . . .

No, unless a retired person lives in splendid isolation atop a remote and inaccessible mountain peak, he need not search far to find much that will keep him constructively occupied. Every community in the land has entire galaxies of things that need doing—activities in which the retired individual can engage and involve himself, achieve visible results and thus obtain satisfaction and pleasure from doing them.

Permit me to underline that none of this is intended to say that every—or any—person must leap, with flailing arms and legs, into this, that or another specific form of activity upon his or her retirement. Each individual—as I have sought to emphasize throughout these pages—has his own bents and inclinations, his own personal "mix" or blend of preferred interests, avocations and activities.

Some—perhaps all—of these are defined long before retirement. Which of them the individual can and will pursue—and to what extent he can and will be able to pursue them—are questions no other person can answer. Much—very much—depends on what advance preparation and planning has been done to create firm physical, psychological and emotional bases and provide material resources for the realization of hopes and ambitions and the achievement of aims and objectives.

There is, however, one constant.

Retirement comes after and as a reward for a long period of useful, constructive activity. It is a crossroads, and the individual arrives at it with certain accumulated assets of knowledge and experience.

Unless he is the exception that proves the rules of HCL—the High Chance of Longevity—the retired person has much time, many years, still before him.

L'ENVOI

Few, if any, human beings are born connoisseurs of any-thing. Each individual is the product of his own experience and experiences, and his tastes and preferences are developed and refined through the years.

My hope in writing these pages has been to demonstrate that today, in our present and Affluent Age, more people have a greater and better opportunity to live long and well than ever before in history. I have also sought to show that middle age need not be feared and that retirement does not write *finis* to a happy life and good living.

My point has been to the contrary. I have argued that it is when a person reaches middle age that his tastes and abilities to discriminate, to distinguish between what is good and what is bad, have reached their peak. And I have maintained —and will always continue to maintain—that with middle age comes the opportunity to reap a varied and bountiful har-vest of satisfactions, gratifications and serenity.

I repeat the eminently practical and effective prescription offered by Oliver Wendell Holmes, Sr., to cure the "malady" of age:

First. As I feel that, when I have anything to do, there is less time for it than when I was younger, I find that I give my attention more thoroughly and use my time more economically than ever before, so that I can learn anything twice as easily as in my earlier days. I am not, therefore, afraid to attack a new study.

Secondly. I have opened my eyes to a good many neglected privileges and pleasures within my reach and requiring only a little courage to enjoy them.

Thirdly. I have found that some of those active exercises which are commonly thought to belong to young folks only may be enjoyed at a much later period.

I am—and have long been—convinced that it is when the human being reaches middle age that he really has the expe-rience and ability to savor life, to qualify as and *be* a con-noisseur of the art of living.